Designing the Lush Dry Garden

Designing the Lush Dry Garden

CREATE A CLIMATE-RESILIENT, LOW-WATER PARADISE

FROM THE RUTH BANCROFT GARDEN
by CRICKET RILEY, ALICE KITAJIMA, KIER HOLMES

Photography by Caitlin Atkinson

TIMBER PRESS · PORTLAND, OREGON

Contents

Frontispiece: Golden hour at the Ruth Bancroft Garden.

Timber Press
Workman Publishing
Hachette Book Group, Inc.
1290 Avenue of the Americas
New York, New York 10104
timberpress.com

Timber Press is an imprint of Workman Publishing, a division of Hachette Book Group, Inc.
The Timber Press name and logo are registered trademarks of Hachette Book Group, Inc.

Printed in Shenzhen, China (APO) on responsibly sourced paper

Text and cover design by Lauren Michelle Smith

ISBN 978-1-64326-373-1

A catalog record for this book is available from the Library of Congress.

• TO •

Ruth Bancroft, Brian Kemble, and all the small
acts of gardeners everywhere that benefit
all the living things on the planet we share.

PREFACE

Ruth Bancroft, Dry Garden Trailblazer

Creativity thrives with limitations. This was true for renowned gardener Ruth Bancroft when she started her low-water garden in 1971 at the age of sixty-three. It was also true for us when we launched the Dry Garden Design Certificate Program (DGDCP) in 2021, where we share Ruth's insights and visionary approach to gardening and design, the knowledge gained by all the RBG caretakers over the years, and basic design principles. We also dive deep into the plants that thrive in our region (and most summer dry regions of the world) with very little water. Over the years, we've expanded the program, adding classes and teachers and including students from around the world. As we've taught these programs over the past several years, we realized that these ideas could be helpful to a wider audience. In creating this book, we are hoping to reach people beyond program participants and inspire them to practice this more sustainable way of gardening.

The Ruth Bancroft Garden

The Ruth Bancroft Garden (RBG or The Garden) is a small botanical garden in a medium-size suburban town in the San Francisco Bay Area. Composed of three-and-a-half acres, RBG is a collection of low- and very low–water plants that are well adapted to the inland summer dry climate. Ruth Bancroft designed it as a personal garden, and it became a public garden in 1994. Today, RBG is a nonprofit and open to the public year-round. It also has a retail nursery, hosts private and community events, and offers a large array of both in-person and virtual classes for children and adults, as well as landscape design services for people wanting to transition their gardens to be more climate resilient. All of these departments support RBG financially and help spread its mission of sustainability.

As the program director at RBG, Alice oversaw the education department, including adult, visitor, and children's programs. The primary focus for this role is to ensure RBG's

Opposite: Autumnal colors announce the fall season at RBG with agave and California native buckwheat taking center stage.

mission is shared in a variety of offerings ranging from lectures and hands-on workshops to webinars and community events. Cricket created the design services department and, as its director, oversaw the landscape design services team. These designers help homeowners create low-water gardens throughout the Bay Area. For several years, Cricket was also one of the primary instructors at RBG.

Together, we started talking about the certificate program in 2019. We knew we had a lot of useful knowledge about dry garden design from both RBG as well as gardens that we've designed for homeowners in our community, but we weren't sure how to structure it into a course or make it available to the widest audience.

Then the pandemic struck. Suddenly everything closed and RBG was scrambling for income. How could we (as an institution) engage people in our mission while being physically separated? We began offering online classes, and had a captive audience who, for better or worse, had nothing but time. What a perfect laboratory. We started to develop classes for everything we could think of. Some were really popular, and others fell flat, but after a year we had a pretty good idea of what people were interested in as well as what they needed to know—but maybe didn't know that they needed to know. So, in March 2021, we launched the first Dry Garden Design Certificate Program.

While we are not immune to the emotional weight of the shifting climate, we believe that we have to take it as an opportunity—a call to action—in how we garden. By gardening for where you are, with plants that will do well with the least amount of intervention, you (we!) can play a small part in righting the ship. Gardening creates habitat, sequesters carbon, makes the gardener and the visitor feel good, and engenders beauty. Gardening is an act of hope. So, with that in mind, we hope this book inspires you to be creative within the limitations of your environment. If we each do something, it most certainly will add up.

—Cricket Riley and Alice Kitajima

Forever Saving Water

I grew up in the 1970s during Marin County's notorious drought. Being the child of earth-conscious (read: hippy) parents, a brick permanently lived in our toilet tank, our neighbors flaunted trendy brown lawns, and "Save Water" stickers plastered our car bumpers. Besides turning off the faucet while brushing our teeth and keeping a five-gallon bucket in the shower to collect the warm-up water, our family—like many others at the time—was hyperfocused on conserving resources.

Today in California, I still hold on to that feeling of living through the "water depression," and I'm the self-appointed water policewoman of the house. A bucket lives in our shower, our thirsty lawn left eons ago, and our garden gets watered sparingly. Even when designing gardens for clients, I strongly encourage removing lawns and adding more unthirsty and climate-appropriate plants that are easy to care for.

When I learned that Alice and Cricket wanted to write a book about the RBG's Dry Garden Design Certificate Program, and highlight gardens both influenced by Ruth's low-water and climate-resilient principles, I was in.

Did my enthusiasm erupt because I already preached the word of low water? Yes. Was it also because as a garden writer, one of my goals is sharing the important stories and lessons of fellow plant enthusiasts? Most definitely. But the real needle mover was that I grew up visiting the Ruth Bancroft Garden with my garden-loving parents, and I have early memories of seeing Ruth puttering around the beds. I also remember entering through the charming green folly and wandering through the adjacent plant-filled greenhouse and meandering grounds. I remember marveling at the massive agaves, tipping back my head to take in the towering palms, crouching low to discover prickly patches, all the while thinking, what are these plants?

Now, of course, palms, succulents, and Mediterranean plants are familiar go-to's in my design arsenal, as most do well here, plus they are reliably attractive, thankfully resource conserving, and some are truly masters in multitasking (low water + low maintenance + pollinator friendly). But as a long-term and mildly obsessive student of nature, I know that I still have much to learn, even much more to fail at and recalibrate, so this is exactly why I visit and revisit RBG.

Every time I wander the winding paths, I gather and squirrel away inspiration (and, of course, reality checks of just how big some beauties can actually get) and then lean on these lessons in my designs and in my own garden. And though my own garden is small, I try to harness the big magic that bubbles up from RBG, whether it's certain choice plant combinations, clever rock placement, or just the ethos of tapping into what gifts and limitations a garden holds. I also think about Ruth's unwavering dedication to observing, experimenting, and learning. My wish is that all gardeners continue to ask questions, be creatively personal and curious, and allow the love of plants and gardening to grow.

—*Kier Holmes*

PART

• 1 •

Designing a Climate-Resilient Garden

Introduction

. . .

GARDENING WITH RESILIENCE IN MIND

Climate change, climate warming, atmospheric rivers, (deep breath) sustained freezes, freak snowstorms, devastating droughts, extreme heat, and heavy rainfall. All these terms and realities of unstable and severe seasonal weather patterns are unfortunately becoming familiar and, potentially, routine to us. This also means that these new norms have embedded into our thoughts, conversations, even worries. And yes, they have moved into our gardens. With our plants and gardens undoubtedly affected by changing and morphing weather patterns, what are we to do? How and to what level do we need to adapt to this variability? Or rather, how much do our plants need to prepare and adapt, and how can we help our gardens get ready for what inevitably lies ahead?

These are hard questions. And helpful answers lay ahead. But first. . .

There's Always More

Yes, planting unthirsty plants is a positive game changer. However, in light of the erratic weather patterns and an altering climate, a lack of water is not the entire dilemma. While this book was being written, *another* atmospheric river barreled down, as agencies issued constant flood alerts and our local reservoirs filled to the brim. For some gardeners, this brought confusion. Why stress about conserving water when apparently we had enough, or even more than enough? With these bizarre and increasingly common weather patterns, some people thought that those of us on the West Coast were out of the woods and could go back to planting water-guzzling turf and tender annuals. This is out of the question; while all the rain is regenerative and helpful to some degree, it doesn't mean we won't continue to experience summers of excessive heat, repeated winter deluges, and unprecedented freezes. How do we respond? The solution is to create gardens that require less but give more. We need to create gardens of resilience.

Gardening with Resilience Means Gardening for Tomorrow

What exactly is a resilient garden? In the upcoming pages, we go into depth regarding this gardening approach, but in general, a resilient garden is one that is in sync with your regional environment. Why is this important? The simple answer: our gardens are integral to a much bigger picture, not just our backyards or individual horticultural ideals. Gardens have major impacts ecologically because ecological gardens that fare well in troubling times inspire awe and wonder, which influences prevailing style trends, which influences more gardeners.

Our goal is to help and walk you through the necessary steps to creating a resilient garden of your own, and provide handy information and positive inspiration. We have curated case studies of attractive, beautifully resilient, and earth-friendly gardens for you to gain inspiration and learn from. Ultimately, we are here to change perceptions of what climate-appropriate, low-water gardening looks like.

Aloe 'Creamsicle' in full bloom under a mature *Aloe* 'Hercules'

How to Use This Book

If you're anything like us, we know that you appreciate a helpful layout of what's to come. In the first part of the book, we discuss the various design styles of dry, climate-resilient gardens, and present a handful of common design principles and lessons practiced and trialed by Ruth and the design services staff of RBG. We then share a selection of essential plants that have proven to be standouts in a waterwise, climate-conscious garden. We discuss the ever-popular container gardening and rewarding tricks to growing in small spaces. We'll walk you through the basics of soil, boulders, irrigation, hardscape, lawn removal, and the tools we can't work without.

It's important to note that the information in this book grew out of gardening practices developed in USDA Zone 9a (this indicates regions with winter lows of 20 to 25 degrees Fahrenheit or -6.7 to -3.0 degrees Celsius). The plants in this book do well in this hardiness zone with minimal to no protection from frost in the winter and minimal summer irrigation once established. We suggest that you spend some time understanding the temperature extremes of your area when creating your climate-resilient garden. We've listed some resources in the back of this book that can assist you with that research.

In the second part of the book, we visit fifteen phenomenal gardens in California, ranging from postage stamp–sized spaces to generously sized gardens, all taking cues, plant ideas, and design principles from the Ruth Bancroft Garden. Because naturally, RBG continues to contribute and influence home gardeners and design professionals beyond its own garden walls. How could it not? Just like a good song, a fantastic garden can percolate and deeply embed in your soul. The tones and textures, spines and spaces seep into your consciousness and follow you around, transforming your perceptions.

In these case studies, you'll get to see inside spectacular gardens that are using resources judiciously but are surprisingly lush and textured. This is because the garden designers and homeowners don't see water restrictions as a detriment, a curse, or punishment, but as an invitation to be creative and resourceful. They have taken on the challenge of designing satisfying, thriving, rewarding gardens that gratify our deep desire to help the world, do our part, and nurture nature.

Please keep in mind that this book just scratches the surface of what you need to know for your garden to evolve into climate resilience. You can dig way deeper into all the topics we cover, but our hope with this book is that you will gain a better understanding of waterwise garden plants and the general garden design process you need in order to create a resilient garden. Hopefully you'll learn a garden trick, tip, or idea, regardless of your skill set and knowledge base. You might get answers to questions you didn't even know you had. The point is to be undaunted by failure and continue to be adventurous in your pursuit of creating a fantastic, climate-ready garden. Ruth was undaunted, and we want you to be, too.

Remember that Ruth Bancroft didn't start her dry garden until the age of sixty-three, so it's never too late. She was an avid experimenter and believed that the best way to learn about a plant was to get it in the ground, see how it performed, and record that information. During the 1970s and 1980s, her techniques were far from common, as were her plant choices. When she inevitably failed here and there (as all gardeners do), Ruth took detailed notes and learned as much from her flops as her successes. The takeaway? Instead of fearing the misses, celebrate the successes. It takes time and trial and error to figure out your site and conditions, and it's all part of the wonderful journey that is gardening. We feel

lucky to be able to share these lessons with you and shepherd you through your journey of insightful failures and rewarding successes.

If we put our minds to it and use a bit of observation and ingenuity, together we can usher in a new type of garden filled with vibrancy and care for the earth and its health. We believe these actions will ultimately make a positive impact by supporting wildlife and pollinators, managing runoff, saving water, improving soil, cooling homes, storing carbon, and providing us with awe and joy. We know it's a lot. But we also know it's possible.

So please, read on, dog-ear pages, highlight helpful tips—even bring this book outside while gardening. We totally give you permission to get the pages dirty.

Happy gardening!

CHAPTER

· 1 ·

Learning from the Ruth Bancroft Garden

Some of you may already know about Ruth and her garden—perhaps you have even had the pleasure of visiting the Ruth Bancroft Garden in Walnut Creek or you have read *The Bold Dry Garden* by Johanna Silver, which goes into great detail about Ruth's history, gardening life, and vision. For those of you who picked up this book without prior knowledge of this determined and adventurous gardener, we can't wait to introduce you. In typical Ruth form of being endlessly curious and thirsty for knowledge, there is always something new to learn, whether you're a seasoned dry gardener or a newcomer to Ruth Bancroft entirely.

Born in 1908, Ruth grew up in Northern California, and was the only gardener in her family. She once mentioned that she couldn't remember ever not gardening, even as a young child. Everything from roses to bearded irises to daffodils intrigued her, and as she grew older, her interest in plants and gardening grew exponentially, so much so that later in life, if you wanted to reach Ruth at home, you had to call before 7 a.m. or after 6 p.m. because she worked in her garden all day, almost every day of the week.

The pivotal moment that really jump-started Ruth into a fascination with dry plants came when she first saw and bought a few hybridized *Aeonium* 'Glenn Davidson' at Mrs. Glenn Davidson's yard sale. And although by today's standards this plant is a bit ho-hum, it's important to remember that plants like *Aeonium* weren't readily available in the 1950s. So the question is, what was it about this plant that drew Ruth in? It was the *Aeonium*'s rosette form, the almost impossible symmetry, that inspired Ruth so much. And it makes sense that she would fall for such a graphic shape, as Ruth initially studied to be an architect, an idea she later abandoned due to the Wall Street crash of 1929 and limited job possibilities. It makes sense that Ruth's architectural interests matched up perfectly with the very architectural form of succulents, cacti, and other low-water plants—from one passion another was born.

But here's another piece of the puzzle—you could even call it a star-aligning scenario. Through the 1960s, Ruth dove deeper into dry plants and began collecting a large assortment of succulents, all of them in petite terra-cotta pots that quickly filled up the small greenhouse next to her Walnut Creek home, and eventually a shade house. At the time,

Page 20: Warm weather blooms at the Ruth Bancroft Garden

Ruth and her husband Phil's main property consisted of a walnut and pear orchard but, due to disease, the orchard was removed. In 1971, the last of the trees on the ranch were cut down, leaving a blank three-acre canvas—bare soil, in need of a vision. "Here's a big, empty field," Phil said to Ruth. "Do you want to use this for your garden?"

Ruth Bancroft in her garden

It was perfect timing, because Ruth had amassed a staggering number of potted succulents (more than two thousand) and they badly needed to get in the ground and stretch their legs. But while this blank-slate scenario sounds ideal, Phil specified one condition: they wouldn't dig a new well and they wouldn't dip into city water for the garden. At this time, water conservation or being a waterwise gardener wasn't in vogue. In fact, quite the opposite. Verdant and ubiquitous manicured lawns sprawled out as far as the eye could see. But as a family of farmers, they considered water a precious resource. Whatever garden Ruth created needed to be able to thrive on water from the existing well. So once again, the pieces fit.

A mandatory water restriction might have daunted and debilitated Ruth if it weren't for serendipity—the plants Ruth collected weren't thirsty at all. If Ruth had collected, say, ferns, then this arrangement wouldn't have worked out very well. Ruth's region has a Mediterranean climate, which means the summers produce little to no supplemental rainfall. Coupled with their self-imposed water restriction, Ruth embraced the sustainable idea of creating a completely dry garden. This took much observation and trial and error. Ruth taught herself how to make dry plants happy, how to protect certain plants in her collection from the soggy winter rains and occasional devastating freezes, like the one in 1972 that wiped out most of her garden. And it took help from a dedicated and knowledgeable team that she fostered over the years. Ruth's foresight, fearlessness, and sheer patience with slow-growing plants created the foundation for her notable garden.

It's interesting to know that Ruth started her garden for the fun and enjoyment of it, never holding the idea that she needed to impress anyone. Ruth also never anticipated that people would take such an interest in her garden, that she would provide inspiration to so many people. But she did. Over the years, as more and more plant enthusiasts and horticulturists learned about Ruth and her Walnut Creek garden, she became an iconic figure. In 1988, plant collector and horticulturist Frank Cabot visited Ruth and learned that she had no plans to protect and carry on the garden after she was unable to tend it. And so, Frank created the Garden Conservancy, a nonprofit organization that supports and preserves gardens throughout the US. Ruth's garden became the first preservation project of this nonprofit and officially opened up to public visitors in the early 1990s. Ruth continued to regularly putter and weed in her garden well into her late nineties, until she passed away in November 2017 at the remarkable age of 109. We can't help but think that her curiosity and love of gardening were the secrets to her longevity.

Today, Ruth's garden continues to be a living example of how gardening in tune with your local climate produces very satisfying results. The lessons she learned and applied are applicable to gardens of every size and many styles. The key is to follow her method: plan, try, and learn from your mistakes. Gardening is a journey, not a destination.

A meandering path through cacti and agaves was Ruth's original entrance into the dry garden.

Guiding Principles of the Ruth Bancroft Garden

Ruth made rules just to turn around and break them. What this means for a gardener is that plans and guides and particulars can exist and be extremely helpful in the beginning stages of creating a conscientious and dynamic garden, especially if you are new to this. But your needs for them can change. Later on, as your garden develops and your skills and knowledge accumulate, rules can still be thought of as gently keeping a garden focused and in its functional state. But no one says you can't veer a little, refocus on something unique or a bit daring, and then go down a different, unexpected path. In the end, if a plant, combination, or design decision makes you happy (and it is climate appropriate), then by all means add it to your garden.

The Ruth Bancroft Garden Design Principles were created to be used as a guide to maintain and enhance Ruth's vision for the garden for years to come. And while she developed them as a framework for her garden, many are basic landscape architecture principles.

- Retain and emphasize Ruth's vision of a garden of meandering paths that periodically open to "rooms" of varying sizes and shapes.
- The planting beds should be mounded to enhance drainage and topographical interest, resulting in a naturalistic feel to the garden. Low mounds help to delineate the subtle swale.
- The central pool should continue to serve as an oasis-like centerpiece and counterpoint to the dry landscape of the rest of the garden.
- Maintain a border of larger shrubs and trees to provide enclosure for the garden and separation from the surrounding suburbia.
- Key sight lines should be maintained through the garden, allowing visitors to enjoy the layers of plantings that are a feature of Ruth's garden.

A coning *Encephalartos horridus*

MISSION

The Ruth Bancroft Garden's mission is to preserve, promote, and enhance Ruth Bancroft's world-class collection of water-conserving plants displayed in her exceptionally designed garden, for the education, inspiration, and enjoyment of the public.

Ruth had a passion for bold architectural plants and their juxtaposition against drifts of colorful flowering plants or softly textured grasses and herbaceous plants.

WHAT IS A ROSETTE?

A rosette is a circular arrangement of leaves or petals reminiscent of a rose. The repetition of this plant shape provides a rhythm and unifies RBG.

RUTH'S FAVORITES

While Ruth's plant interests were generous, she had a special place in her heart for certain genera and families including *Agave*, *Yucca*, *Echeveria*, and other Crassulaceae.

- Maintain a number of small and larger trees to provide dappled shade for the plantings that demand less than full sunlight, and to create deep pools of shade as a counterpoint to the bright, open expanses with their more desertlike feel.
- Waterwise and water-conserving plantings are critical components of the collection.
- Intellectual curiosity should always inform any expansion in the plant collection.
- Group plants according to their similar cultural needs, not according to their country of origin.
- Plants should be arranged informally within curving pathways and soft-edged beds.
- Avoid any straight lines in the plantings and rock placement.

- Beds should be assembled in layers, from ground covers to midsize shrubs and larger succulents to trees of varying canopy heights.
- Continue the emphasis on repeating the rosette form in varying sizes and colors.
- Use odd numbers of plants in group plantings rather than even numbers to enhance the sense of a naturalistic setting.
- Plants should be maintained with a recognition of their natural character and not highly manicured.
- Place emphasis on structural pruning over purely aesthetic for the purposes of health and vigor.
- Remove plants no longer serving a valuable role at RBG.

HOW TO GET DRAMATIC COMPOSITIONS

Use contrasting color, texture, form, or foliage. Example: Plant a moody *Leucadendron* 'Ebony' or *Aeonium arboreum* 'Zwartkop' next to a silvery *Agave ovatifolia* or *Aloe brevifolia*.

Meet Brian Kemble: The Ruth Bancroft Garden Curator

You won't find Brian battling sleepless nights worried about whether Ruth and her garden will continue to inspire local and distant gardeners or garden designers. Brian says, "No one needs to worry about that. People will always be inspired." So where will you find Brian, especially if he's not traveling to Mexico or South Africa to study and photograph plants in their native habitats? Certainly you'll catch him plant patrolling, snapping photos of what's blooming, teaching classes at RBG, and being the official torchbearer.

Ruth and Brian were kindred spirits, sharing a mutual love of all things leafy, petalled, and colorful—even those wielding spikes. Ruth's daughter, Kathy, once told Brian that he was the botanical son that Ruth always wished she had.

Brian credits his maternal grandfather, the green thumb of the family, for passing this plant passion on to him. He spent his childhood in Hawaii, and at ten years old took a random hibiscus cutting and simply stuck it in the ground. Miraculously it took root and grew into a healthy plant. This improbable success embedded in Brian a vast sense of possibility.

Years later, Brian went to college to study philosophy and the history of Buddhism and Hinduism—surprisingly not botany or horticulture. Upon graduation, Brian knew two things for certain. One, he simply couldn't go and get a job at the local philosophy store, and two, he still had no idea of his career path. So he packed up and moved to San Francisco. "It was here that I started noticing all the wonderful succulents growing around, like *Graptopetalum* and *Pachyphytum*, etc. I started growing these on my windowsill because they were easy to grow from a leaf or cutting and their leaves were fat and cool and came in wonderful pastel colors."

Brian Kemble, curator of the Ruth Bancroft Garden

A couple of years later, Brian's trajectory changed even more when he fortuitously became the neighbor of landscaper Charles Grimaldi (for those who think that name sounds familiar, yes, a *Brugmansia* is named after him). Charles hired Brian to help him out with garden installations. Charles would take Brian to meetings of the Cactus & Succulent Society in Oakland, introducing him to other prominent plant people in the Bay Area like Victor Reiter Jr. (who was a leading light in the California Horticultural Society), Lester Hawkins at Western Hills Rare Plants Nursery, and Wayne Roderick at Tilden Regional Parks Botanic Garden.

Now immersed in a plant-obsessed community, Brian focused his fascination and eventually became the vice president of the Cactus & Succulent Society of California, where he coordinated speakers for the monthly meetings. One of their speakers was Clive Innes, owner of Holly Gate Cactus Nursery in southern England and, when he arrived, Clive told Brian that he had heard about a succulent garden in Walnut Creek and would like to visit it. Brian said sure, and off they went to Walnut Creek to meet Ruth.

This was in 1979, and Brian had never heard of this garden, which at that point was seven years old and still Ruth's personal garden. And while the plants were still quite young, Brian was impressed with the scale of what Ruth had created and very much liked her chosen plant groups, especially the agaves and echeverias. Ruth and Brian hit it off right away as fellow plant nuts, and he gave her his name in case she might be looking for hired help. The next year Ruth asked if he would take care of the greenhouse one day a week.

Ruth kept her succulents in a greenhouse before she started what is now the Ruth Bancroft Garden (she also grew a more traditional English-style garden around her house with roses and irises). She used the greenhouse for propagation and to protect her more cold-sensitive specimens. Brian's success in his role led Ruth to build a bigger greenhouse so that Brian would have more room to continue hybridizing aloes and propagating a vast collection of succulents. After several years, the plants that Brian hybridized became part of Ruth's main collection, making them a dominant feature at RBG. More importantly, Ruth and Brian's relationship grew, matured, and blossomed. They got each other excited about new plants, and their love for leaf, spine, and flower became contagious.

After Ruth's passing in 2017, it became Brian's role to preserve RBG while simultaneously guiding its adaptation to changing weather patterns and the incorporation of new

Aloe 'Creamsicle'

BRIAN'S NOTABLE HYBRID PLANTS

Working with the extensive collection at RBG, Brian has created many hybrid aloes, agaves, gasterias, and cacti. Some of these have found their way into the plantings at the garden, adding unique touches not found anywhere else. The garden serves as a laboratory where they can grow into mature specimens and be evaluated for their horticultural qualities. Some have come into wider use after being introduced into nursery trade, like Aloe 'Hellskloof Bells'.

Aloe 'Creamsicle'
Aloe 'Hellskloof Bells'
Agave parrasana ′ × *A. colorata*

Opposite: Contrasting leaf and flower color create a dynamic composition.

plant introductions. Brian and garden manager Walker Young both strive to maintain Ruth's vision while also being aware that gardens are constantly evolving works of art. Together, Brian and Walker stroll the garden weekly, making lists of tasks for the horticulturists, deciding what to prune and how, marking if something needs removal and what should replace it, discussing anticipated conflicts and next steps for the garden. With a collective goal, both Brian and Walker always fall back on RBG principles to inform their choices and the future. According to Walker, Brian has stood patiently and persistently as a guardrail against any design ego, shooting down ideas if he finds them inconsistent with what he knows Ruth would have wanted.

When Brian adds new plants to the garden, he isn't thinking about keeping things exactly as they are forever. Instead, he imagines a scenario where he shows Ruth these new plant choices and sees if she is interested and would add them to the garden. Brian shares what goes through his head. He wonders, "If Ruth knew what we know now, would she have done this?" Ruth remains Brian's guide. Of course, he's imagining her voice, but it's safe to say that Brian has a solid idea of what plants would've caused a sparkle in Ruth's eye and put a smile on her face.

CHAPTER

• 2 •

Laying Out a Design

When you hear the words "low water," do parched visions of withering brown leaves, cracked dirt, and spiny cacti speckled through a barren desert landscape enter your head? Perhaps. But that perception changes when you visit the Ruth Bancroft Garden, where you can wander the wide, meandering paths and witness a remarkable tapestry of color, texture, pattern, and rhythm. It's almost as if Ruth painted with plants, brushing the landscape with different hues, shapes, and textures. You witness a waterwise wonderland filled with statuesque cacti, broad-leaved aloes and agaves, and charming grass-skirted yuccas.

Ruth, of course, was a gardening pioneer, and her garden became a beacon for water conservation during the 1990s when California faced epic drought conditions. Today, her garden continues to model waterwise design while also inspiring sustainability by highlighting regionally appropriate plant palettes. It not only matters what you plant, but where you're planting it; Ruth taught that one must grow alongside the natural rhythms and patterns of the garden's site itself. Making climate-appropriate plant choices reigns supreme—the right plants set the garden and the gardener up for success.

COMMON MISCONCEPTIONS ABOUT DRY, CLIMATE-RESILIENT GARDENING

- Plants are poky, spiky, and harsh.
- Gardens are flat, stark, and sparse, with few flowering or leafy plants.
- Areas are void of creatures, except for the occasional darting lizard.
- Native plants are scraggly and dull looking.
- Sharp, white rocks cover the ground, acting as glaring icing.
- Plants require no supplemental irrigation.

REALITIES OF CLIMATE-RESILIENT GARDENING

- Plants can be soft, wispy, bold, and lush.
- Gardens can be mounded, layered, dramatic, and blooming.
- Pollinators and wildlife can abound.
- The color tones can be verdant, saturated, and bright.
- Wood or gravel mulch should be used to insulate the soil and plant roots but never be the focal point of the garden.
- Plants require irrigation until established, which is usually two to three years, but can be longer, depending on weather patterns.

Page 32: The lush and inviting dry garden of Molly Stone in Berkeley, California

Top left: Cycads, aloes, euphorbias, and mesembs in a garden bed at RBG

Top right: The colorful leaves of *Echeveria*, golden oregano, and scented geraniums give this garden year-round interest in a design by Cricket Riley.

Above: Succulents and palms in AJ Kallet's modern hillside garden

Left: *Agave*, *Aeonium*, *Grevillea*, and *Dorycnium* provide color and texture in a Bay Area garden by Kelly Kilpatrick.

Why Garden with Climate Resiliency in Mind

Gardening is known to be good for positive mental health and well-being. The act of gardening, and spending time in outdoor spaces, makes a person feel hopeful and positive while also relieving stress. A garden, regardless of size, is a place of respite, where friends and family connect, and a space to enjoy the seasonal rhythms. Adding to that, a thoughtful, well-designed garden boosts the experience by stimulating and soothing all the senses.

In part spurred by the pandemic, many people are now maximizing their garden spaces, seeing the potential of outdoor rooms and recreational areas. This means the focus rests on making gardens more comfortable and livable, rather than redoing a yard solely for curb appeal. People are also, luckily, aware and concerned about judiciously using resources, keeping in mind the climate where they live. This is where climate-appropriate and -resilient gardening enters the scene. Planting this way means using plants well suited to the weather conditions of the location. For example, in California (like other Mediterranean climates where there is little to no summer rain) gardeners should choose plants that do not require excessive irrigation in the summer, and, in places that experience hard frosts, gardeners should avoid plants that need protection. For our climate here in the inland San Francisco Bay Area, there are many plants that fall into this category, such as native sages, yuccas, and aloes. In fact, all the plants listed in this book need minimal summer watering and are cold hardy if planted in the proper conditions. It's important to research regions across the country and around the world with similar cold, heat, and water conditions to your own to help find good plant candidates for your climate-resilient design.

Australian native, *Banksia praemorsa* (red-form)

There are many benefits of planting this way, not least being the conservation of resources (water, fertilizers, labor), the financial savings (less inputs mean less investment), and positive environmental impacts. But ultimately, by starting from a point of resilience, you spend more time enjoying your garden and less time struggling to keep it alive.

We use the terms "climate appropriate" and "climate resilient" interchangeably when talking about plants, but climate resiliency goes beyond just what plants you use. It involves how you place the plants in your design, and your choice of hardscape, mulch, and irrigation. All these choices grow a stronger garden that can both survive and thrive as our weather patterns intensify.

Some say gardening in a thoughtful, climate-resilient way is the "right" thing to do. Others claim it's the "only way." But whatever your reason for adopting a waterwise and climate-resilient garden, we assure you that the outcome will be a positive, conscientious, and earth- and pollinator-friendly garden.

Site Analysis

The first thing to do is get a lay of your land, thinking big but also realistically. If you're a designer working with a client, consider sending an evaluation form with important questions for them to thoroughly think about before you meet. If you are working on your own space, going over these questions will help you better understand how to tackle your project. Here are some examples of questions from the Ruth Bancroft Garden Form.

- What space are you thinking about landscaping? Specifics are good here: front yard, backyard, or whole property?
- Briefly describe your project. Much like the act of journaling, sometimes the act of pen to paper (or fingers to keyboard) helps work through thoughts and solidify emotions and wants.
- Do you have any favorite or must-have plants? Now is a good time to peruse your collection of garden books to jog your memory of certain long-forgotten favorites or plants you've been obsessing over but never committed to. You can also go for walks in your neighborhood, scroll through Pinterest, or visit a local nursery. Even if the plant or look you want isn't appropriate for the garden, substitutions can often be easily found.
- Do you have any preferred colors or a design style? Here is where a Pinterest board or a "vision board" comes in superhandy. Construct a virtual or actual collage of colors and garden images. The more images you can come up with, the better. It really helps to define the look of the garden early. Additionally, once you have those images, take a little time to write down what you like about them. People see different things when they look at the same picture. Articulating what you like and why will make getting something similar much, much easier.
- What is your project budget, realistically? This is understandably one of the most difficult questions for people. But being honest with yourself upfront allows you to design to the budget. It doesn't do you any good to design a garden you can't afford to put in.
- Do you have a project timeline? Remember that things usually take longer than wanted or expected due to material availability, weather, and work schedules. In general, give yourself at least six months to complete a project.

Classifying Your Wants Versus Your Needs

Next, it's time to consider how you currently use the outdoor space and how you or your client plan to use it moving forward. This is a good time to classify and rank the "wants" and "needs" for the new garden. For example, a client might want to grow their own food, but they'll need to be realistic about their bandwidth for this type of upkeep.

Think about the purpose of your garden. How will the space be used and what will it do or provide? Should certain features be highlighted, views blocked, and entertaining spaces created? To help work through both the design and budget process and to ensure that all ideas are on the table, it is essential to be clear about what is a "need to have" and what is a "would be nice." Here are some features to consider including in a garden design:

- Planting area(s)
- Edimentals (plants that are both edible and ornamental)
- Natural swimming pool/pond
- Vegetable garden
- Cutting garden
- Compost area
- Potting bench
- Dining patio
- Lounge area
- Water feature
- Firepit
- Dog run
- Garbage area
- Service yard
- Storage
- Laundry line
- Play space
- Greenhouse
- Hot tub

An unconventional play space in a modern garden in Santa Barbara

Clockwise from top left: Lounge area, Water feature, Garbage area, Vegetable garden

Recording Your Site Conditions

The next step in the design process is to take inventory and measurements of the existing site. This recording process is called site analysis. Whether you draft a base map yourself, purchase a GIS basemap, or get a professional survey, it is important to walk the space and take notes and an inventory of your site's existing elements, including slope grade, soil, sun pattern, existing plants, property lines, fence lines, existing hardscape, windows, doors, views, and utilities. The most successful end result will require the understanding of the garden's condition, site-specific details, and environmental factors. At a minimum, note the following:

- Is the property large or small?
- What are the built elements; in other words, what is currently there, what is staying, and what is going?
- Measure the space and record the topography. Is it flat or sloped? If sloped, in what direction?
- Note the views from the house. What do you see when you look out from inside?
- Note how the house sits relative to the garden and the street.
- Note where the doors, windows, and built elements are, including water spigots.
- Observe the borrowed view. What do you see beyond the garden, and should this view be preserved?
- Are any plants staying? If so, mark their locations.
- Record the soil. Is it rocky, clay, loamy, or sandy? Dig down six to twelve inches for a orphan.
- Where do the trash cans live and what is their route to the curb?
- Consider your electric and gas lines. Important: before any digging begins in the US, always call 811 to get the lines marked.
- Record existing irrigation systems and location(s) of valves.
- What should be screened and hidden, if anything?
- Should items be framed on the property? Are there existing focal points or features on your property that you want to highlight, like a large specimen tree or a view of the house?
- Record the sun, shade, and wind patterns at various times of day. When is the garden most sunny? Least sunny?
- Record water-related issues. Are there signs of runoff or flooding?
- Are deer, rabbits, and/or other small mammals a nuisance? Is this a seasonal issue or pervasive? Also, do you plan to keep out the deer eventually or give them free rein?

- What outdoor activities happen and how will the space be utilized?
- Notice the natural flow in relation to where people (and pets) walk. This is called the "desire line" or "goat path." Making note of it in advance prevents future disappointment when you discover that your dog has a favorite lounging spot or route.

VALUE ENGINEERING

Most people can't afford to have every feature they want in their garden. Value engineering is figuring out ways to cut costs while still retaining some of the things you want. Can't afford a poured-in-place firepit with a gas line? Attractive propane models exist. Also consider gravel as a great patio material, as it's much cheaper than pavers or concrete. Buy fast-growing plants in small sizes (though plants are usually the cheapest part of the project). Consider working with a designer to figure out where to save and where to splurge, such as on statement plants and good soil/irrigation.

A bird's-eye view of a hillside succulent garden showcases mature specimens and flagstone paths and patios.

Additional Factors to Consider

Along with soil and water, other important factors must be considered, such as the aspect, exposure, and microclimate of a garden. These determine where you place your plants for practical and visual effect, such as a tree for shade, a large shrub for wind protection, a sculptural succulent to view out a window. These factors will determine how happy certain plants will be, and you want to set them up for success.

ASPECT

Aspect can refer to two different concepts. The first is the view; when you look out a window into a garden, this is the aspect. The second is the position of the garden in a particular direction. For example, in the northern hemisphere, a south-facing aspect is sunnier and north-facing is shadier. Both are important to consider for both the design and the health of the plants.

EXPOSURE

When speaking about exposure and plants' tolerance to the sun, the following terms are used: full sun, part sun, part shade, and full shade. The exposure of a garden will determine what plants to plant and where. In a north-facing garden that gets full shade, you want to plant things that will be happy in these conditions. In dry shade situations we like to use *Aeonium* spp., *Heuchera maxima*, or *Ribes viburnifolium* because they require very little irrigation once established, thrive in low light, and have nice, dense habits and long boom times, despite the light conditions. Conversely, in gardens with full, all-day sun, we love to plant *Hesperaloe* spp., *Sphaeralcea* spp., and *Muhlenbergia rigens* because they need the heat and sun to bloom and put on their spring and summer show. Keeping the exposure needs of the plant in mind will allow you to specify plants that will not just survive but thrive in your garden with minimal intervention, which in turn lowers your carbon footprint and makes your garden more resilient.

MICROCLIMATE

Microclimate refers to a highly local, site-specific climate and its subsequent temperature, exposure, and moisture conditions, which may differ from the general regional climate. Microclimates can exist because of such things as buildings (which can cause conditions such as heat islands, deep shade, or wind protection), topography (such as a low spot where cold air can settle), and existing plants (like trees that change the way the sun hits the garden). Every region experiences different weather, which affects microclimates in varying ways. Within the Bay Area alone, vastly different heat, cold, and moisture ranges exist. Even within a particular garden multiple mini-microclimates can exist.

Choosing a Garden Theme or Style

Once all the details about your garden are observed and written down, the process becomes a bit more creative. You're ready to think about a theme for the garden.

WHY CHOOSE A GARDEN THEME OR STYLE?

Garden themes create unity and a cohesive space. With a determined theme, your garden will look intentional and not random and haphazard, even if the goal is to create a design that's a bit more rambunctious and naturalistic. When thinking of a theme, it's nice to complement the inside and outside of your house, neighborhood, and local environment.

A shimmering *Brahea* 'Super Silver' in front of Ruth's Folly

Garden themes give guidance to the specific layout and maintain a strong point of view and focus. By offering paired down choices and more constraints, the project feels less daunting and overwhelming, so you can make more thoughtful decisions. They also can help reduce work and maintenance tasks in the garden because your wise plant choices will require less upkeep to thrive. You won't waste time buying plants that might struggle and require tending to that you can't keep up with.

HOW TO DECIDE ON A GARDEN STYLE

To design a garden style, you should base your choices on personal preference or past experience with plants and gardens. A garden should reflect your needs, interests, and lifestyle—not that of your friends or neighbors, what social media is hyping, or what's trending. Ask yourself, what do I want to do in the garden? Maybe you want to spend long afternoons pruning and tending to your plants, or perhaps you want a low-maintenance garden that looks good all year with minimal care. Or maybe you want to entertain more or simply relax in a hammock and read books. Then, consider the style of your neighborhood. This mainly applies to the front yard. Do you want your garden to blend in or stand out and make a statement? Also consider the architecture of your house and how you can complement its design features.

REALITY CHECK

Remember to only install a garden that you're willing to devote routine time and effort to, either by you or a hired professional. A garden is an investment and requires proper attention and skilled maintenance to keep it healthy and thriving. Otherwise, it wastes time, materials, and resources.

Consider the microclimates. Within some gardens multiple microclimates exist, some with drastically different areas due to factors such as solid fences, trees, surrounding buildings, and light exposure. Take advantage of these mini-microclimates by choosing plants adapted to these various conditions and create a more diverse ecosystem. Remember to check light exposure, temperatures, and moisture in each distinct area.

Always keep in mind that the styles described below are just a starting point. You can create your own climate-appropriate garden theme. Consider a waterwise jungle or a woodland retreat. You can even create a design based on your favorite color. The only requirement is to decide and define what you want the end result to look like before you begin so you have some parameters.

Five Climate-Resilient Garden Styles

While many different garden styles exist, here are five that work well incorporating low-water, summer dry plants. Remember that choosing a style is just a starting point. Many gardens don't fall completely under one specific style but instead mix multiple ideas together. The bonus of selecting just one style, however, is that the focus helps organize your thoughts, gives them purpose and direction, and, most importantly, eliminates things that don't belong. Many other garden styles exist beyond the ones we'll cover in this section. Beforehand, there are some important considerations.

Constraints are limitations that serve to create a better end result. For example, the wish for a contemporary garden filled with tons of color might clash, style wise. So even if you adore color, if you know that a contemporary garden is really what you want, then limit your color palette early to make both the process and the result better.

And say you want a tropical garden. Pick plants with oversized leaves and rich greens, then densely layer them. If you fancy a traditional garden, use a limited palette, and choose naturally tight-formed plants and plant in straight lines. Practically any garden style can be achieved if you thoroughly consider form, layout, and texture, and then use low-water plants adhering to those specifications.

THE CALIFORNIA COTTAGE STYLE GARDEN

Opposite: Flowering California natives in a Santa Barbara garden by Topophyla

The cottage garden is inspired by English gardens overflowing with blooms and blossoms, with color year-round. The feeling is lush and relaxed, without a trace of formality. The style highlights soft, fine textures and supports a casual look and feel. In the California

cottage style, meandering paths wind and weave, and the occasional bench, arbor, sculpture, or even a birdbath tuck in between the blossoms. For a welcoming front yard, consider adding an open feeling rustic wood fence and some boulders, maybe one or two flat-topped ones perfect for resting on. California natives mixed with generously flowering plants from other summer dry regions like Australia, South Africa, or the Mediterranean can be balanced with succulents that add year-round interest. The keys are bountiful blooms, generous amounts of color, and soft, relaxed texture.

This garden style complements many different architectural styles but works best with medium to small traditional style homes. It's important to note that the California cottage garden style is high maintenance, so be prepared for copious amounts of pruning and deadheading, and routine mulching.

PLANT IDEAS FOR A CALIFORNIA COTTAGE GARDEN

Trees: *Arctostaphylos manzanita* 'Dr. Hurd', *Ceanothus thyrsiflorus* 'Snow Flurry', *C.* 'Dark Star', *Cercis occidentalis, Chilopsis linearis*

Shrubs: *Myrica californica*, *Osmanthus* cv., *Rhamnus californica*, *Romneya coulteri*

Low Shrubs: *Achillea* 'Moonshine', *Diplacus aurantiacus*, *Epilobium canum*, *Salvia* 'Hot Lips', *Trichostema lanatum*

Ground Covers: *Bulbine frutescens* 'Hallmark', *Ceanothus griseus* var. *horizontalis* 'Diamond Heights', *Eschscholzia californica* 'Buttermilk', *Stachys byzantina*

Below: Add a few big, coarsely textured agaves for a dynamic element, or mix in smaller varieties of succulents for a higher level of texture and interest. Also, consider choosing native cultivars bred to perform more reliably in home gardens. Here, charming California buckwheat and a clumping agave act as highlights in the native section of RBG.

Below right: California native, *Chilopsis linearis*

Clockwise from top left: *Osmanthus cv.* (shrub), *Epilobium canum* (low shrub), *Bulbine frutescens* 'Hallmark' (groundcover)

Mammillaria, golden barrel, and *Opuntia* in a garden bed planted by Ruth in the early days of RBG

THE DESERT GARDEN

The desert garden is inspired by how plants grow naturally in arid landscapes and focuses on a naturalistic feel with a good dose of negative space. In this style of garden, plants are intentionally placed, taking center stage and becoming living sculptures and individual focal points. For visual success, remember to embrace a controlled palette. Also, incorporate some form of shade and filtered light, either from trees, palms, or shade structures. Add a cooling water feature to bring balance and to reference the oasis. To top a desert garden style off, use gravel as mulch and naturalistically place boulders/rocks with plants nestled in them.

While some may think desert gardens are all spines and cacti, this style can highlight soft and floriferous elements. For example, *Hesperaloe*, *Baileya*, and *Sphaeralcea* all work well in a desert-style garden, and they are very leafy and bloom for long periods in the warmer months. Desert gardens complement modern, ranch, or adobe-style homes of all sizes, and are a low-maintenance option. Depending on the number of shrubs, you can maintain a desert style garden with quarterly or biannual tending.

PLANT IDEAS FOR A DESERT GARDEN

Trees/Palms: *Brahea armata, B. clara, B. edulis, Cercidium ×'Desert Museum', Prosopis glandulosa*

Tall/Screening Shrubs: *Agave americana* var. *marginata, Cereus peruvianus, Cleistocactus strausii, Trichocereus pachanoi, Yucca rostrata*

Shrubs: *Agave parryi, Echinocactus grusonii, Opuntia violacea* var. *santa-rita, Salvia apiana*

Ground Covers: *Aloe* 'Safari Rose', *Arctostaphylos uva-ursi, Delosperma* 'Fire Spinner', *Mammillaria geminispina*

Opposite, clockwise from top left: *Cercidium* ×'Desert Museum', *Echinocactus grusonii, Trichocereus pachanoi, Aloe* 'Safari Rose'

THE SPANISH REVIVAL/MEDITERRANEAN GARDEN

The Spanish Revival/Mediterranean garden is a common sight in summer dry California, but ultimately inspired by walled Islamic gardens. This style appeals to all the senses, with fragrant plants and gurgling fountains. You'll always find a place to sit and socialize, often protected from the sun. Hardscaping is often wood, stone, terra-cotta tile, and gravel. This garden style complements Spanish Revival architecture but also works well with any other architecture style, and requires medium maintenance. To help the garden look its best, plan on trimming back and cleaning up at least four times a year.

Italian cypresses flank the front door of this classic Spanish Revival home.

PLANT IDEAS FOR A SPANISH REVIVAL/ MEDITERRANEAN GARDEN

Tree/Palms: *Butia odorata, Cupressus sempervirens, Olea europaea, Quercus agrifolia*

Tall/Screening Shrubs: *Cycas revoluta, Laurus nobilis, Nerium oleander, Rhamnus alaternus* 'Variegata', *Tecomaria capensis*

Midsize Shrubs: *Agave* 'Blue Glow', *Lavandula ×intermedia* 'Alba', *Pelargonium tomentosum, Salvia clevelandii*

Ground Covers: *Origanum vulgare* 'Aureum', *Rosmarinus officinalis* var. *prostratus, Teucrium cossonii, Thymus serpyllum*

Clockwise from top left: *Olea europaea* (tree), *Nerium oleander* (tall shrub), *Origanum vulgare 'Aureum'* (groundcover), *Agave 'Blue Glow'* (mid-sized shrub)

THE CONTEMPORARY GARDEN

A contemporary garden takes its starting point from the mid-twentieth-century modernist movement that proliferated after World War II, while also incorporating current design ideas and trends. The feeling is often calm with a restrained design and color palette. Clean lines, simple forms, and a repetition of plants are common with this style to create a sense of order and balance. Plants and hardscape act as sculptural elements while also mirroring the surrounding architecture. Stone, steel, concrete, and hardwood materials are commonly used. Owners of mid-century modern houses easily default to this style due to its natural partnership between contemporary garden designs and modern architecture, but contemporary gardens complement almost all styles of architecture. Low to medium maintenance, depending on the plant palette, this style may require quarterly or biannual tending.

A soft, contemporary garden in Southern California by Pamela Burton and Company

PLANT IDEAS FOR A CONTEMPORARY GARDEN

Trees/Palms: *Acacia podalyriifolia, A. stenophylla, Aloe 'Hercules', Platanus racemosa*

Tall/Screening Shrubs: *Acacia iteaphylla*, *Banksia praemorsa*, *Leucadendron* 'Safari Sunset', *Pittosporum tenuifolium* 'Silver Sheen'

Midsize Shrubs: *Agave ovatifolia*, *Lomandra* 'Lime Tuff', *Muhlenbergia rigens*, *Protea cynaroides* 'Mini King'

Ground Covers: *Banksia repens*, *Carex divulsa*, *Dichondra argentea* 'Silver Falls', *Dymondia margaretae*, *Grevillea* 'Austraflora Fanfare'

Clockwise from top left: *Aloe* 'Hercules', *Acacia iteaphylla, Carex divulsa, Agave ovatifolia*

THE RUTH BANCROFT–INSPIRED GARDEN

As discussed, in the Ruth Bancroft–inspired garden, form, foliage, and texture come before flowers, but, of course, a striking inflorescence is always welcome. Mounds are prevalent, borrowed views highlighted, paths and beds blend seamlessly, and boulders anchor spaces with fortitude. This style offers a playful sense of hide-and-reveal as you journey through the space, always wondering what fantastic plant lives around the next corner. The Ruth Bancroft–inspired garden is high maintenance, as a highly diverse plant palette requires much care. Be prepared for a minimum of monthly maintenance.

Golden hour at RBG

Drafting Your Site Plan

The first step in putting a garden design on paper is drafting a site plan, which is basically a map of your property as it currently exists. This can be created by hand or with a computer-aided design (CAD) program. Many resources are available to help you create the site map, from county records to Google maps, from quick online site map companies to professional surveys. Whichever route you take, it's good to double-check the measurements for accuracy and adjust as needed. Also, remember that the plan needs to be created to scale and easy to read.

THE BUBBLE DIAGRAM

Once your site map is created, ask yourself: Where should the different elements of the garden sit? What is the best way to move through the space from one area to another? How can I fit what I want into the space and take into account the different factors that may affect these decisions? To answer these questions, begin drawing bubble diagrams to try out different layouts and think through the best scenario, while not committing too much time to the actual drafting. The benefit of a bubble diagram is that it allows you to quickly work through the location and flow of your garden design without getting hung up on the details.

To draw your bubble diagrams, use drafting tape to secure your base map to a table. Then place a piece of tracing paper on top of it and trace where the building or street sits. This will allow you to move your tracing paper and easily return it to the same place. We like to buy rolls of 12-inch tracing paper because it works with both 8.5 x 11-inch and 17 x 11-inch paper, but you can find tracing paper for whatever size you commonly work with. Once you have a permanent structure marked as your anchor, quickly draw circles or amorphous blobs to indicate the different features you are going to include in your design. Show paths or common trajectories with arrows. Don't get hung up on neatness and remember the bubbles shouldn't resemble the shapes of the objects in real life. They are simply placeholders, as this is an exercise to quickly move through ideas and see how all your desired features can come together in your design. Try out different combinations and think through the advantages or disadvantages to each arrangement. It's common to have multiple bubble diagrams for the same design.

You'll notice in the following two bubble diagrams by landscape designer Nikki Vroom that the same features exist in the design, but their placement is different. Additionally, by noting some specific site conditions, such as wind, views, etc., you can further evaluate the best placement for these elements early in the design process.

Bubble Diagram 1

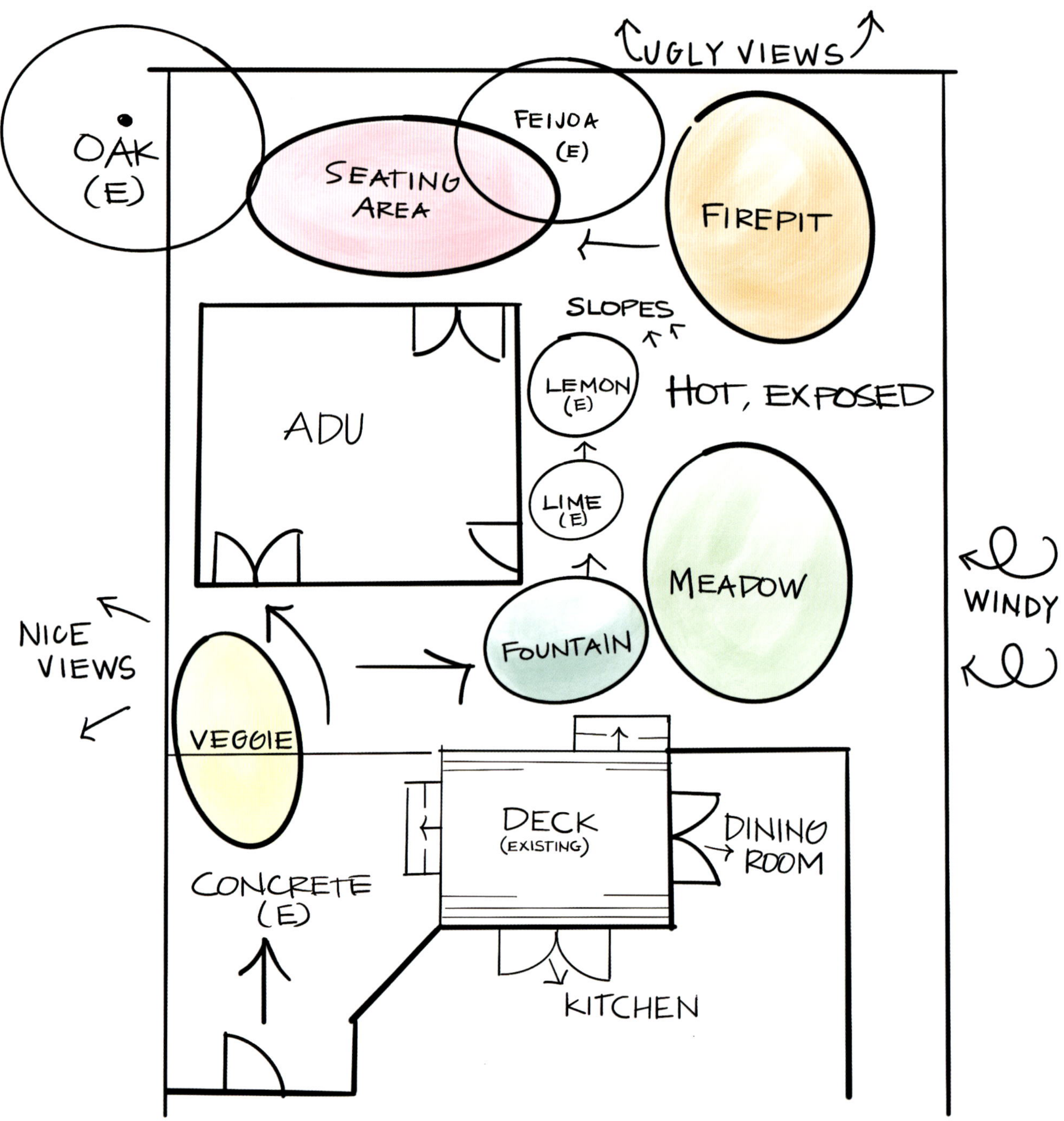

Bubble Diagram 2

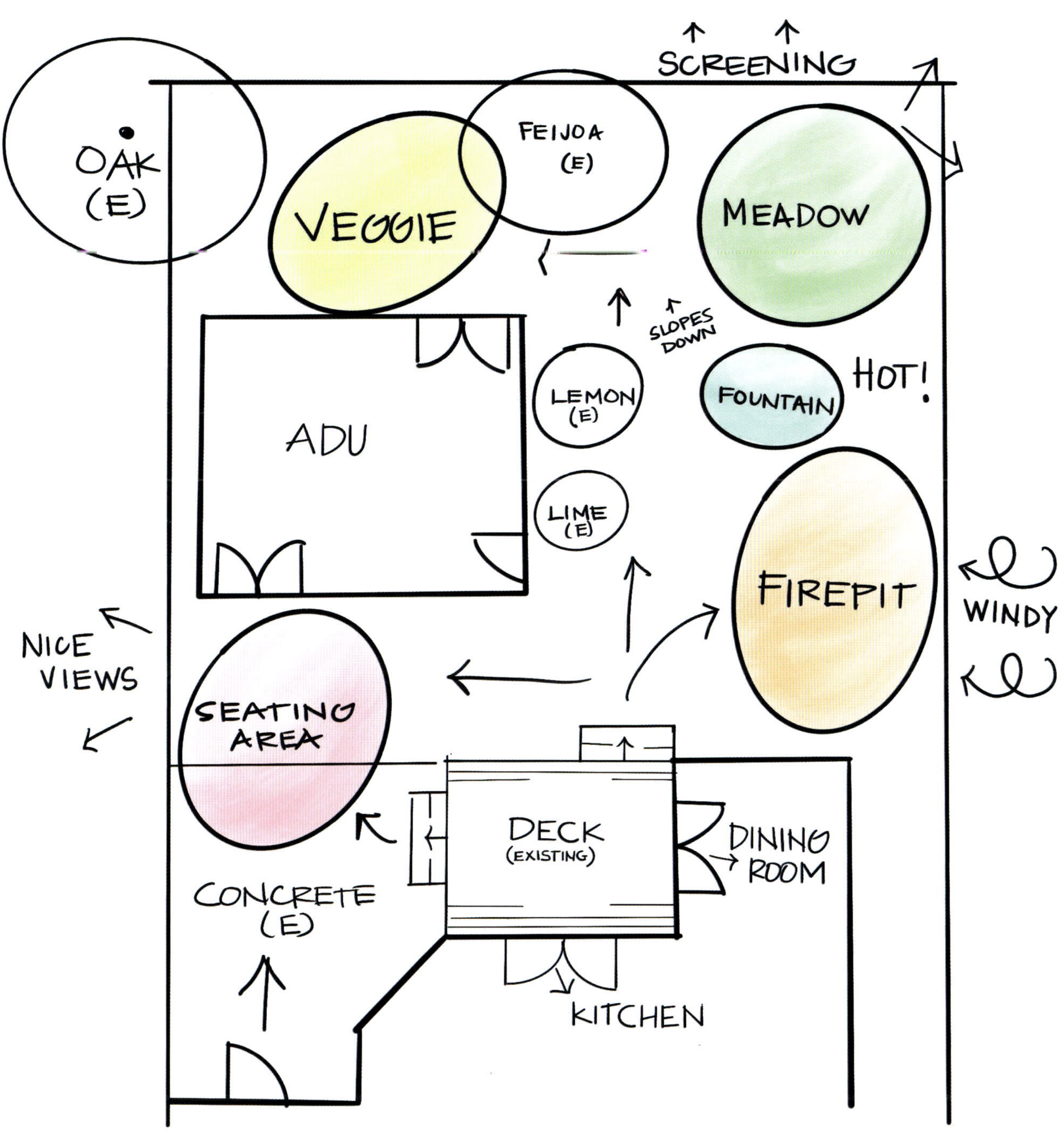

Considering Proportion in the Layout

Proportion refers to the relationship between one element and another in a composition. It compares sizes, shapes, and quantities. Understanding proportion and composition takes time and practice. College courses, studying other designers' work, and trying things out yourself can all help refine and grow your understanding of what makes for a successful garden layout. Here are several key points to consider as you develop this part of the design, regardless of what shape it takes.

PATIO SIZE

In general, patios shouldn't be smaller than twelve feet across. You want to be able to push out a chair or walk around the perimeter. Of course, instances will occur where there is only room for a single chair or a pair of chairs and a café table. But if you have the space, it's good to consider not just the footprint of the furniture, but also how you might move through and around the area.

PATH SIZE

A path should be at least three feet wide. This allows for one person to walk comfortably through the space. If you have ample room, a five-foot path is even better, as it allows two people to walk side by side through the garden, and it creates a feeling of ease.

BED SIZE

In smaller spaces, keep beds no smaller than three feet deep. There are some instances where this isn't possible, but if a bed is going to be less than two feet, consider not having a planting bed at all.

In larger spaces, think about making bigger beds rather than a bunch of small beds with paths in between. Bigger beds are healthier for plants, can create plant communities, and it's a more pleasant experience for people in the garden. This was something that Ruth learned herself through trial and error. The first beds she laid out were fairly small, but as the plants grew, she realized that the flow of the paths and the layout of the "rooms" would feel better if she combined them into larger beds. Plus, the plants really needed the extra space!

FLOW

Flow is one of the most important things to consider when initially coming up with your garden design. The flow is both the layout of the spaces/activities (patio, grill, clothesline,

A wide path allows groups to gather in the Ruth Bancroft Garden.

driveway, front walk, etc.) and the way the spaces are connected. The bubble diagram is superhandy when figuring out this element. Thinking about how you will use the space and what activities work best close to each other (e.g., compost by vegetable beds, trash cans close to the driveway, patio with a good view) will help you create a functional and successful garden.

TRANSITIONS

It may seem obvious, but it's important to work out how the new design will integrate with the existing structures. When you step out the back door, how are you going to enter the new space and what will you see? When someone parks in front of the house, how will they get to the front door and what will that journey be like? Additionally, think about how you will move from one space to another in the garden. You want smooth transitions within the design as well as between the new and existing elements.

A combination of lavender, grasses, olives, and other plants complement the Spanish-style home.

SIGHT LINES

Think about what you see not only when you look into the garden from the house or where your eye is being directed when in the garden, but also those views beyond your property line. These can be things you want to screen or things you want to accentuate.

Taking Shape with Form

A garden layout can take on many different forms: curvilinear, circular, rectangular, rectilinear, diagonal, angular, arced, or tangential. In many home gardens that we design and install, we use some form of a curvilinear or rectilinear layout. A rectilinear design is highly efficient for fitting the most elements in a space, and it works well in a wide variety of garden styles, including contemporary, desert, Spanish Revival, and traditional. You can also easily interrupt the straight edges with plant material, making it feel softer, if that's what's desired. A curvilinear design evokes a relaxed, casual feel that is suitable for many home gardens and is often used when people want cottage, naturalistic, or informal gardens. While it ultimately comes down to personal preference, there are certain factors that can help in the decision process.

CONSIDERING ARCHITECTURE

Surprisingly, the architecture of the house doesn't predetermine the shape a garden will take. While we often see modern houses having rectilinear gardens or storybook Tudors surrounded by curving paths and beds, these two could easily swap and the gardens would work equally well.

CONSIDERING GARDEN STYLE

Like the architecture of the house, garden style is also very subjective. In a cottage garden, the obvious choice would be to create winding paths, but you could just as easily plant soft, billowing borders along straight paths.

CONSIDERING EXISTING HARDSCAPE

This is one of the most important factors to note when selecting a form. If some of the existing hardscape elements work, incorporate them into the new design. This is good for both your budget (hardscape is one of the most expensive parts of an installation) and the environment (the old hardscape needs to be dumped and the new hardscape needs to be produced). With this in mind, the existing hardscape you choose to keep should help determine the shape and the flow of the new hardscape elements.

CONSIDERING YOUR DESIRED FEEL

Like existing hardscape, thinking about how you want the garden to feel is key in the decision-making process. Do you want lush, casual, formal, or wild? Consider what feeling you want the garden to evoke and then work toward that in your design. For example, if you really like formal gardens, you'll probably be happier with a rectilinear design. If you want something casual or wild, then curvilinear will be better. Plants can give a space personality, but the layout is the base structure that provides the foundation of the design.

A variety of palms create a tropical feel around a natural swimming pool.

Here are two concept plans created by Nikki based on Bubble Diagram One. One is rectilinear and the other curvilinear. Both plans reflect the layout of the same bubble diagram but communicate a different feel.

Rectilinear

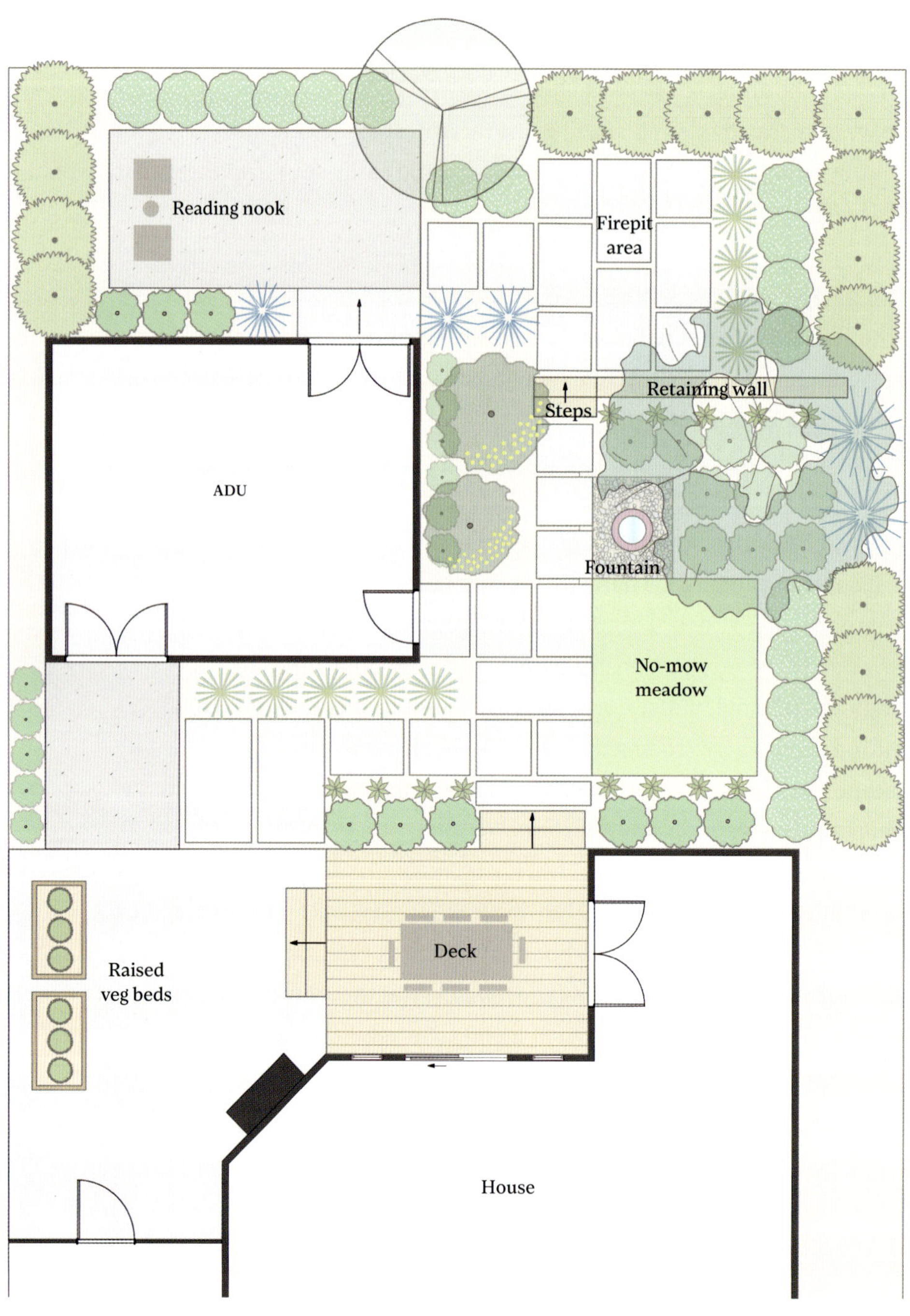

Curvilinear

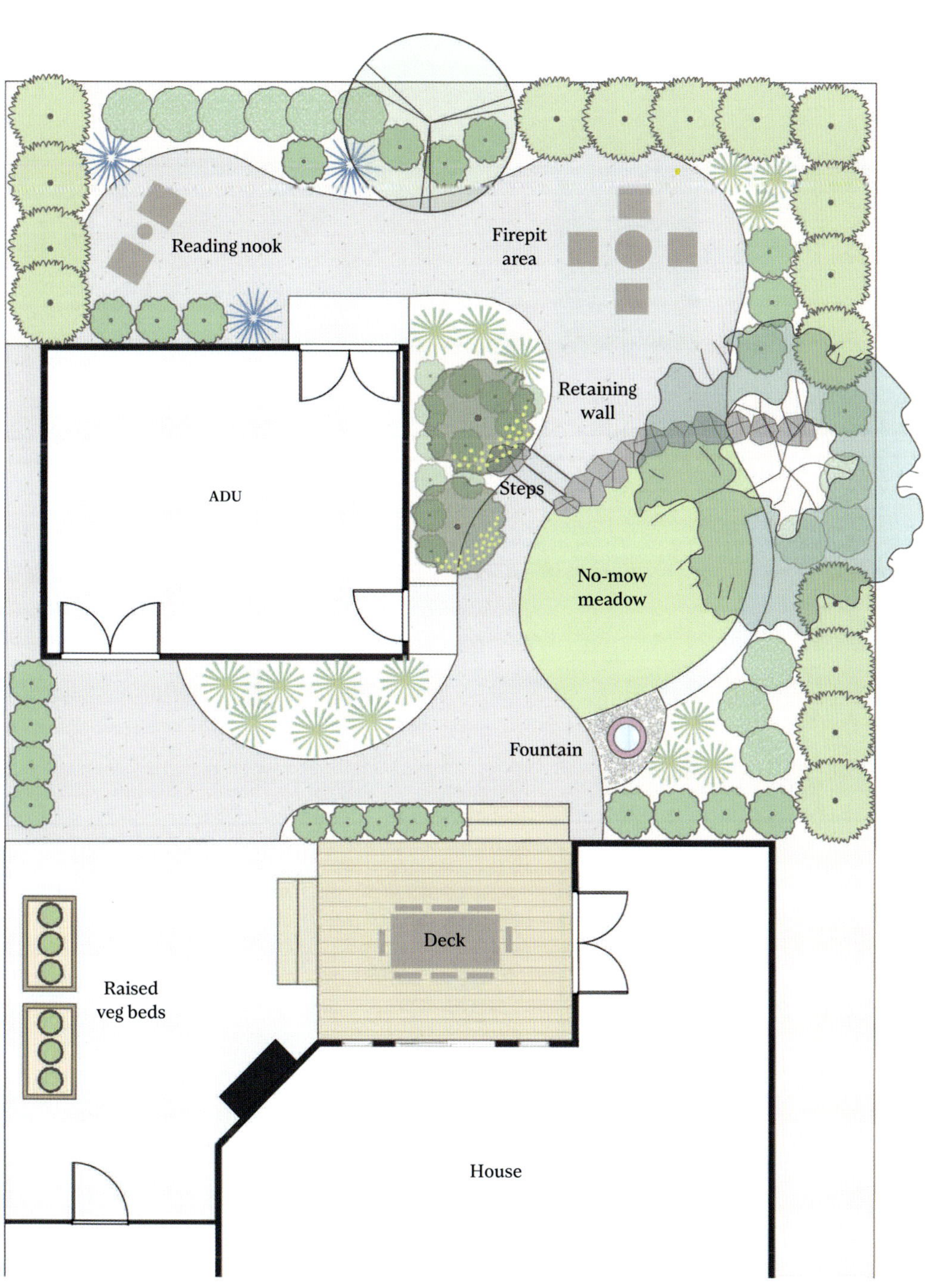

HIDE-AND-REVEAL TECHNIQUE

When laying out the paths on your plan, show your visitors a target or an end goal, then momentarily screen it from view as they continue their approach. Finally, reveal the end goal a second time from a different angle or with an intriguing new detail. The purpose is to make the journey more interesting and the arrival more rewarding, like a visual gift.

Above: A curving path draws visitors though the Northern California garden of Cricket Riley.

Left: Create rooms by using ground covers as the floor, midsize plants as the walls, and arching tree branches as a living ceiling.

Color Theory and Planting Design Concepts

Earlier, when discussing garden styles, we touched on the idea that plant choice greatly contributes to the overall look of the garden. In this section we look at some design concepts that will help you develop a planting palette that achieves the look you desire. Again, these are just guidelines and their purpose is not to constrain but rather to help you make design decisions.

THINK OF THE GARDEN LIKE A PAINTING

Technically (and romantically) your garden is a living work of art. How will you go about painting it with plants? Naturally, you can start by thinking about your favorite hues, but sometimes it's also helpful to know a bit about color theory (a visual tool for understanding color). By understanding the basics, you can better understand why certain color combinations work and why some seem jarring. Also, an understanding of color theory can help you combine different colored flowers, bark, and foliage. Of course, once you get the gist, you can hold on to some as truth and push aside those not to your liking.

Left: A layered and colorful composition with *Echeveria gibbiflora* hybrid, *Agave desmetiana* 'Variegata', *Anigozanthos* 'Landscape Lilac', and *Atriplex lentiformis* in Cricket Riley's garden

Right: Vibrantly colored leaves give year-round interest in this composition at RBG.

Color Wheel

This diagram shows the relationship between primary (red, blue, yellow) and secondary (purple, orange, green) colors, and the shift from light to dark value.

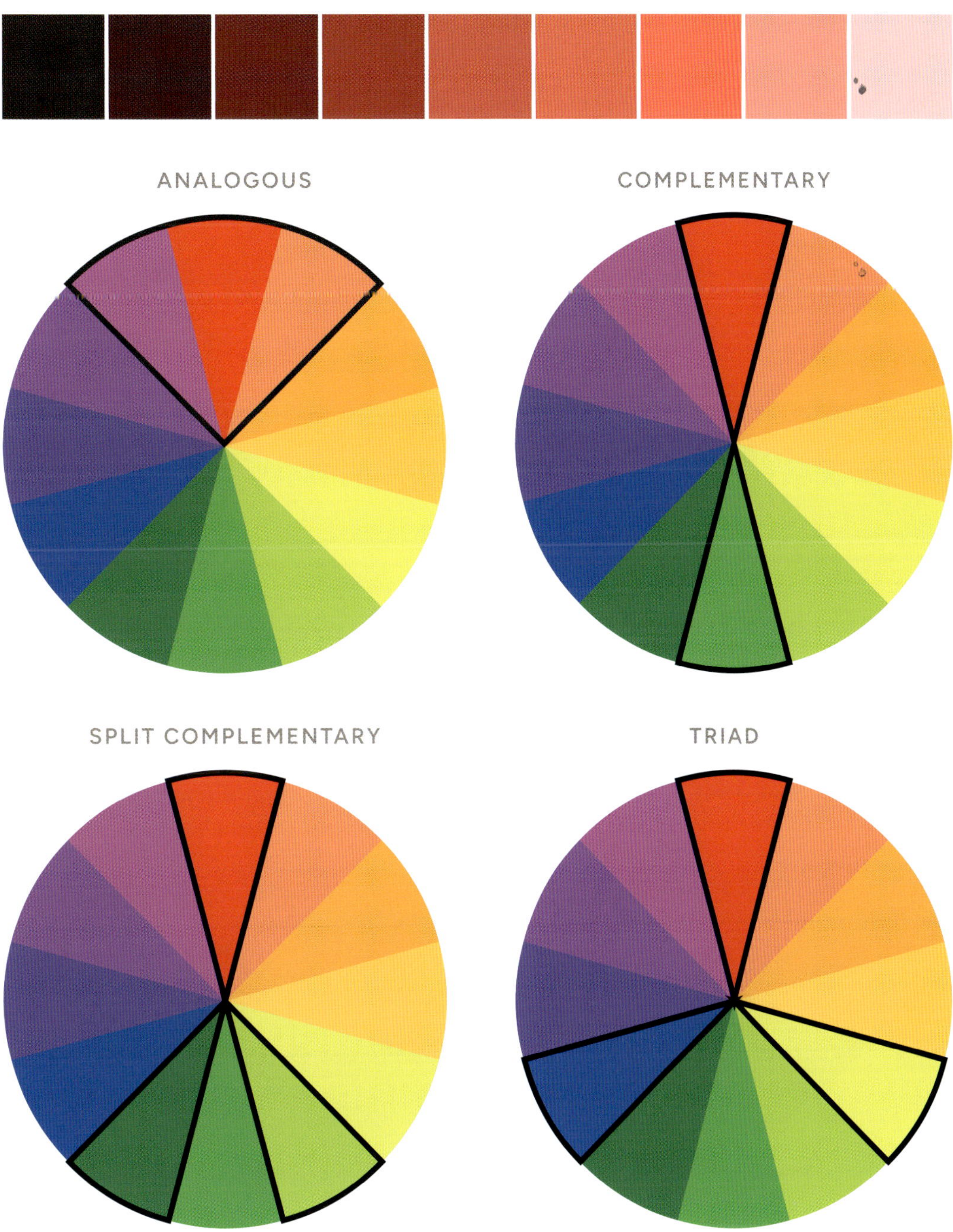
MONOCHROMATIC
ANALOGOUS
COMPLEMENTARY
SPLIT COMPLEMENTARY
TRIAD

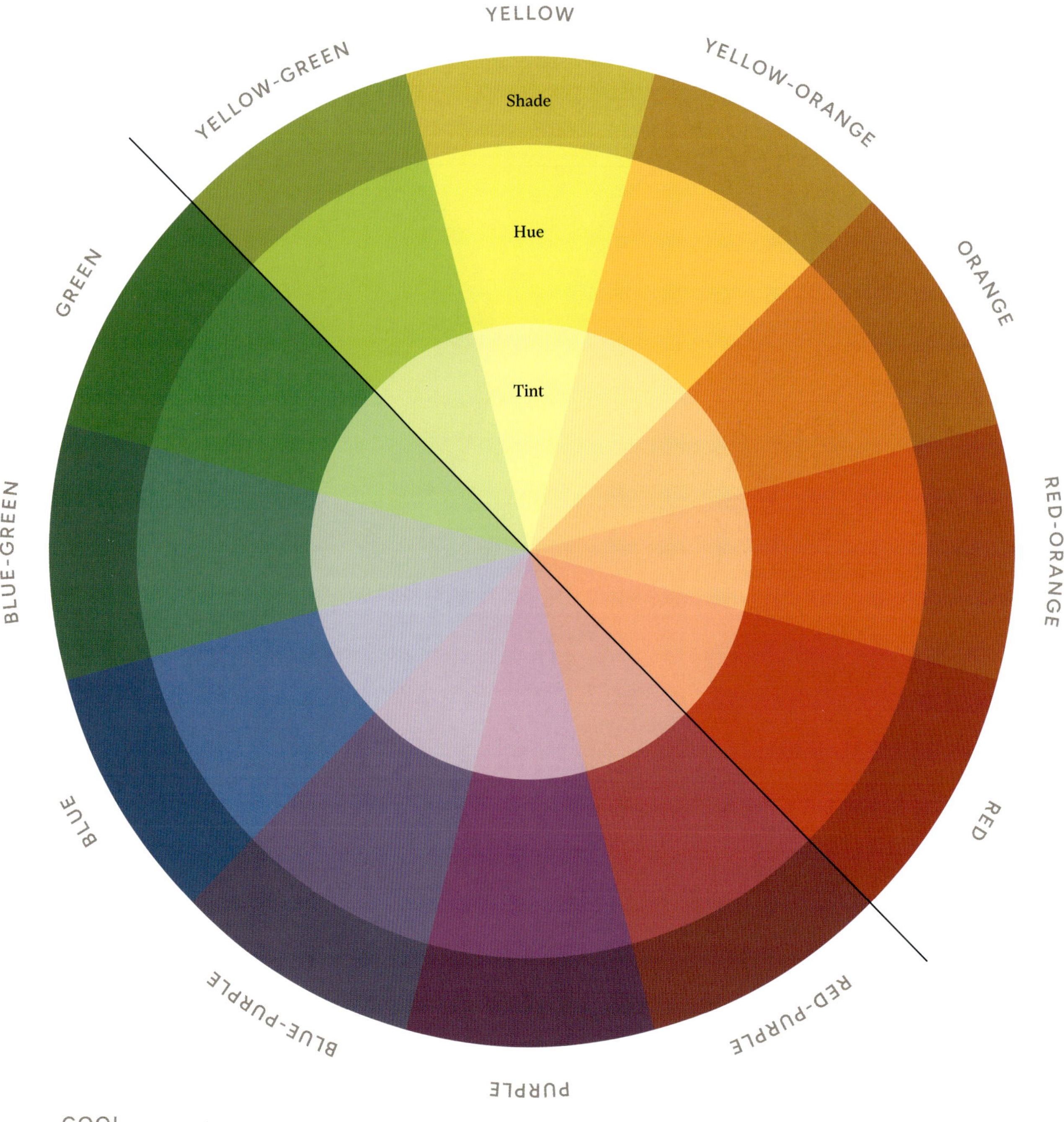
WARM
YELLOW
YELLOW-GREEN
YELLOW-ORANGE
Shade
Hue
Tint
GREEN
ORANGE
BLUE-GREEN
RED-ORANGE
BLUE
RED
BLUE-PURPLE
RED-PURPLE
PURPLE
COOL

COLOR TRICK

To make a small garden feel bigger, use cool colors. To make a big garden feel smaller, use warm colors. Cooler colors recede and warmer colors come to the forefront. Additionally, warmer colors command more attention, so use them sparingly if you want a relaxing garden.

The basics of color are *temperature* (warm or cool), *contrast*, and *schemes*. Obviously, no right or wrong choices exist when it comes to picking colors in the garden, as this step is purely a matter of personal taste. For some, a riot of color is the preferred look for a more energetic mood, while others gravitate toward a hushed, calmer palette. But remember, color schemes are more successful when applied uniformly throughout a design, so decide what colors you will be using and stick to them. Additionally, colors have more impact when there is repetition, so group plants in drifts (multiple specimens of the same plant planted in groups) for maximum effect and appeal.

Start by deciding what temperature you want your garden to be: warm and energetic (yellows, oranges, and reds) or cool and soothing (blues, greens, and purples)? A warm palette is often lovely in colder climates and a cooler palette in a warmer place. Regardless of your choice, a good rule of thumb is to never have more than 30 percent warm tones. Warm tones are very visually engaging and can distract from the subtler elements of the design.

Do you like complementary colors—colors directly opposite each other on the color wheel? When used next to each other, complementary colors have an intensifying effect, like these combinations: yellow with violet, green with red, and blue with orange. Remember, when thinking about the colors of plants, be sure to think about both the leaf tones and flower hues.

An analagous arrangement: *Achillea* 'Moonshine', *Asparagus densiflorus* 'Myers', *Santolina rosmarinifolia* 'Lemon Fizz', *Lomandra* 'Breeze', *Westringia* 'Wynyabbie Highlight', *Bambusa multiplex* 'Alphonse Karr'

COLOR SCHEMES

For a simple but striking combination, use analogous (or similar) colors close to each other on the color wheel, and try to keep the color intensity similar, such as pairing red with orange, orange with yellow, yellow with green, or violet with red.

Do you like just one color? This is called a *monochromatic* theme. The feeling is discrete and subdued with a restrained color palette. If this is your flavor, remember that differences in plant textures and form become key elements to keep the scene interesting and ensure the composition doesn't feel flat.

Incorporating three colors evenly spaced on the wheel is a *triad*, such as violet, orange, and green, or blue, red, and yellow.

Or, you could start out with a complementary couple like yellow and violet, but then use colors nearby on the color wheel, such as red-violet and blue-violet, to split the complement to yellow. This is called *complementary* or *split complementary*.

Don't forget about neutral colors (gray, white, and black) or earth tones (tan, olive, and brown). Both create solid backdrops and help heighten other colors while also adding a visual pause between different color themes.

Opposite: Complementary colors: *Encephalartos lehmannii* 'Kirkwood' and *Echeveria gibbiflora* (purple form)

Below left: Triad: *Ferocactus* sp. and *Baileya multiradiata*

Below right: Monochromatic: *Lessingia filaginifolia* 'Silver Carpet', *Bismarckia nobilis, Acacia iteaphylla, A. podalyriifolia nobilis, Acacia iteaphylla, A. podalyriifolia*

VARIEGATED LEAVES

You can always add variegated plants to a shady area to lighten and brighten up a gloomy space. Some great choices include *Aloe cameronii*, *Cotinus coggygria*, *Crassula capitella* 'Campfire', *Heuchera* cultivars, *Leucadendron* 'Hawaii Magic', *Sedum nussbaumerianum*, *S. rupestre* 'Angelina', and *Yucca gloriosa* 'Bright Star'.

Clockwise from top left: *Sedum nussbaumerianum*, *Sedum rupestre* 'Angelina', *Cotinus coggygria*, *Leucadendron* 'Hawaii Magic'

MAXIMIZING VISUAL INTEREST WITH TEXTURE AND CONTRAST

Flowers are wonderful, but they can be fleeting. Interesting foliage, however, brings year-round appeal to your garden. To ensure your garden has perennial visual interest, think about incorporating different textures and contrasting shapes and forms through the leaves, bark, and branches of your plants.

Creating contrast between two plants placed next to each other allows the viewer to differentiate between the two and enjoy how they interplay, as well as possibly give the eye a chance to rest. With contrast, individual plants also stand out more. Like color, there isn't one strategy or one correct way when you're playing with texture and contrast.

When designing a garden, two kinds of texture exist: fine (thin and wispy) and coarse (wide, larger leaves). For instant intrigue, pair up and contrast fine foliage with bolder, coarse leaves. As with most things, moderation is key. Try maintaining a balance of mixed textures. Consider one-third coarse texture combined with two-thirds fine. For a tropical look, increase the number of coarse-textured plants and decrease the fine textured.

Finely textured plants are lovely viewed up close and add movement to a garden, but too many together can look blurry. Consider *Lomandra*, *Verbena*, and *Teucrium*.

Coarse-armed plants like cacti, agaves, and yuccas can offer a strong visual element and tame a mass of blurry foliage. Plants with soft, fine leaves add movement and play with the light, like *Bouteloua gracilis* 'Blonde Ambition' and *Muhlenbergia rigens*. For a low-water tropical look, think about selecting plants with oversize dark-green leaves, such as *Strelitzia nicolai*, *Brahea edulis*, and *Pelargonium tomentosum*.

Cricket's three favorite plants flourishing in her garden: *Pelargonium* 'Chocolate Mint', *Brahea calcarea*, and *Atriplex lentiformis*

Right: Bold broadleaf plants add weight to a garden and are the perfect foil for fine or feathery foliage, just like this *Agave* with *Eriogonum*.

Above: Gray foliage excels at making other colors pop, for example, *Dudleya brittonii* and *Dorycnium hirsutum*.

Left: A collection of boldly-textured plants create drama and interest in a small entry bed.

PLANT PLACEMENT MATTERS

Guidelines exist for how to place plants based on how the eyes interpret information, as well as on sound horticultural practices. In nature, plants appreciate growing next to each other, so keep this in mind when placing your plants and avoid laying them out like polka dots. It's fine to have space in between your plants, but they will be happier if they can touch and create their own environments. Here are some helpful starting points to consider:

Layers and Groupings Think about how the eye will move through the planting and make it interesting. Create layers and groupings and avoid planting one-offs of small growing plants, as this will look jumbled. Also, vary the color and texture to create definition in your layers. Even with a restrained palette, consider the placement of plants in relation to their neighbors to create a dynamic composition.

A repetition of rosettes in a garden bed at RBG

Above: *Agave attenuata, Aloidendron barberae*, and *Olea europaea*

Above right: A loose pattern with an informal placement can create a garden that mimics nature.

Right: *Leucophyta brownii* and *Chamaerops humilis*

Massing For a modern, contemporary look, plant multiples of one plant, also known as massing. A trick to massing the same plant in rows is to offset the rows, making every other row line up. In more casual or naturalistic gardens, mass plants in waves or groupings. Don't know where to start? Place three of a species together and then two more of that same species a few feet away. Continue to build off this pattern throughout the bed and garden.

Rhythm Repetition is an invaluable tool for creating structure, harmony, and flow in a garden. In general, use odd numbers up to seven because it creates a pleasing visual rhythm. When you plant in odd numbers, the eye moves through the space, and the planting feels more natural.

Wayfaring Place plants in a highlighted position to visually signal the entrance and lead the visitor to a certain desired area. A great example of this is placing a pot or two with large, sculptural plants along a path leading to the front door of a home. Great options for this are *Fatsia japonica* in a shady area and *Chamaerops humilis* in a spot with full sun.

Two *Echium wildpretii* provide wayfaring along a path at RBG.

Specimen Size The size of plants you buy depends on availability and your budget. In general, buy the largest plants you can afford if they are slow growing. If you choose fast-growing plants, consider smaller container-sized plants because smaller plants are easier to plant and less expensive to purchase. Some people also believe that smaller plants develop healthier root systems. For instant gratification, use specimen plants close to maturity, but be prepared for the hefty price tag.

Moderation Avoid the urge to make your garden look full and complete from the start. The downside to the overplanted insta-garden, when you densely plant mature or semi-mature plants, is that it can affect the health of plants, as restricted airflow encourages pests to march in and diseases can infiltrate plants. Then there is the eventual removal of cramped plants. Keep in mind the mature size of the plant when you lay out your design and trust that they will grow that big. A freshly planted garden may look bare initially, but the wonderful thing about plants is that they grow and fill in over time (unlike furniture). If you want impact right away, consider investing in some larger slow-growing specimens and mix in smaller faster-growing species. And don't forget to mulch! Either wood or gravel mulch protects the soil and helps the garden look finished while the plants grow in.

THE IMPORTANCE OF PROPORTION

When it comes to planting design and placement, make sure to consider proportion, the concept of how the size and shape of plants play against each other as well as that of nearby built elements.

When laying out a planting bed, generally place taller plants in the back, medium ones in the middle, and smaller plants up front. However, also consider the different angles and vantage points created by windows, paths, and patios, as well as the scale and the visual weight of all the elements, including the mature sizes of plants. If the bed is approached from multiple angles, the tallest elements should sit in the middle zone and the layering up should happen on all sides. It's important to always consider whether plants will block each other as they grow.

A winding path takes advantage of arching olive tree canopies.

Also remember to add enough plants to provide necessary heft and form to a garden, without overpacking it. Plants are the least expensive part of a new garden design and, as they mature, they become more valuable (unlike a bathroom remodel, which loses its value over time). Also, tricky as it may be, consider how large the plants will eventually get and subsequently look in the space. You don't want to accidentally block views or constantly have to cut branches out of pathways. We often see people plant agaves close to walkways, only to have them grow and block the passage with their large, sharp leaves, which if cut back, ruin the architectural form of the plant. Knowing this in advance, you can place the agave deeper in the bed and let it grow to its full, beautiful potential.

MATURE PLANT SIZE: THINK SMALLER

We estimate three-quarters of the stated mature size when working with plants less familiar to us because a plant's performance is very dependent on the specific conditions of the garden. Some plants will grow beyond their expected size due to favorable soil and water conditions, while others may fail to thrive because of the opposite situation. This is something you won't really know until the plant grows in the garden. So, to hedge your bets, estimate the plant will be happy but not too happy. Fingers crossed.

Finally, consider that 30 percent of new plants may fail in a garden, with some plants taking off while others will struggle. This isn't the fault of the nursery or the gardener, but the nature of working with living things. The takeaway is that every garden is different and unique and, like Ruth, you should try different plants to see what eventually survives and thrives. Ruth didn't initially understand the specific horticultural requirements of some of the plants. Over time, she figured out they needed more drainage or protection from the heat and she was able to amend the soil or alter their placement within the garden. With others she realized they wouldn't thrive in her garden conditions and removed them.

CHAPTER

· 3 ·

Plants for a Lush Resilient Garden

Ah, wonderful plants. Not only do they emit oxygen, they are also beautiful, fragrant, and full of potential. When it comes time in the design process to pick your plants, the creative mind naturally explodes with countless potential and possibilities. So many choices, so little time, and likely even less garden space.

The biggest takeaway for success in plant selection is that the best plants for your garden are the ones already adapted to your climate. When you start to narrow down your plant list, the mind inevitably starts asking questions. Is this the right plant choice? Will this survive here? How is it going to eventually look? This is normal. And one of gardening's perks is that most plants are not difficult to remove if they aren't happy where they are. A garden is an evolving creation and never officially complete.

As we touched on earlier, plants are the paint for your garden canvas. And being able to select from a broad palette makes the garden design exercise even more fun. In the following sections, we will share some of our favorite plants. These are plants we commonly use either at RBG or in gardens we design for other people. They are well adapted to thrive with little intervention and minimal supplemental water once established in areas with hot, dry summers, like those we experience in the inland Bay Area, as well as our colder, wet winters and predominantly clay soil. In other words, these are our climate-resilient top picks. With that in mind, when you start selecting plants for your plan, research your choices based on where you live and your climate by visiting local public gardens and nurseries, as well as investigating the horticulture resources at your local schools and universities.

USDA Hardiness Zones

In 2023, the US Department of Agriculture released a new version of its Plant Hardiness Zone Map, which hadn't been updated since 2013. At the time of this book's publication, half of the country was bumped up into a category half a zone warmer. While scientists carefully explain that more data will be collected and analyzed before attributing this shift to climate change, we have undoubtedly witnessed and experienced extreme weather patterns in our own gardens. While basic information about your zone is helpful when gathering a preliminary list of potential plants, pay attention to seasonal nuances as well

Page 80: Colorful soft and sharp succulents nestle in boulders at RBG.

Guadalupe Island native *Brahea edulis* flanked by California natives *Arctostaphylos refugioensis* and *Heteromeles arbutifolia*.

as microclimate conditions in your garden. It may be that you live in a microclimate even colder than the technical zone the map says you're in, based on your angle to the sun and whether or not you're in the shadow of a hill. Hardiness zones are the best place to start, but never the place to stop.

A Plant's Native Range

Most people are familiar with the idea of a native plant. But we usually default to seeing plants within a political boundary (like the state of California) instead of their true native range. The California Floristic Province is an area that stretches from southern Oregon into northern Baja California along the coast, encompassing much of California's inland regions. This area is characterized by hot, dry summers and mild, wet winters. It is also a large geographical area with a broad range of microclimates and conditions.

Using this and other floristic provinces as our reference point for what is native is an extremely useful and science-based categorization. But using the floristic province is not enough; we have to look at the specific conditions (wind, sun, fog, rain, soil, to name a few) and the microclimates from which the plants hail. So while we strongly encourage using native plants, understanding the specific microclimate and region that the plant is native to is crucial

Butia odorata, *Quercus agrifolia*, and *Olea europaea*

in understanding whether or not that plant will be successful in your garden. For example, while we in the Diablo Valley are closer geographically to Muir Beach than the coast of Southern California, we shouldn't plant redwood trees (which are native to the north coast of California) because they require a lot of water in warm climates and really struggle in our area as our climate changes. Rather, we should plant Guadalupe fan palms (which are native to Guadalupe Island off of Baja) because they are well suited to thrive in our area based on the climate.

ZONAL DENIAL

Ruth Bancroft occasionally succumbed to this affliction—a deliberate ignoring of plant hardiness or heat tolerance, resulting in a need to protect certain plants in winter or summer. This was certainly the case with her prized *Ceiba speciosa*, which she covered in the winter to protect it from the cold until it was too big to cover. Once that happened, the tree suffered significant trunk damage from a cold winter snap. The tree is still in the garden, with a large gash in its trunk. It is a beautiful tree but not the specimen it would be if it grew in a warmer winter climate. RBG now encourages the use of hardy plants that are also heat resilient.

Essential Trees and Palms

If you are redesigning a garden, or starting with a blank slate, trees and palms are the first things you should select and place in your design. Trees set the style for the garden. Their size and shape and whether they are deciduous (lose their leaves) or evergreen (don't lose their leaves) not only create the structure and framing of the garden, but also help determine the horticultural requirements of the plants that go beneath.

Before adding trees and palms to your garden, remember that time is also an element to factor in, meaning you should realistically consider future growth and ultimate size. If the specimen is moderate to slow growing, and you want impact right away, this is a good time to pay more for a larger plant at the outset.

WHY ADD TREES AND PALMS?

- They help establish the architecture of the garden, creating walls and ceilings.
- They establish areas of shade, acting as a living, natural pergola.
- They create their own microclimates with their canopies. This opens up the opportunity to use different plants in the cooler, more protected areas generated under large trees and palms.
- They can help obscure or hide unsightly views.
- They provide a habitat for beneficial creatures.
- They act as focal points.

Above: *Agave ovatifolia* and *Chamaerops humilis*

Left: As a design element, trunking yuccas can act as trees, as seen here at RGB.

Mariosousa willardiana

Essential Trees

Acacia cognata, *A. podalyriifolia*, *A. stenophylla*
Acca sellowiana
Aesculus californica
Afrocarpus gracilior (syn. *Podocarpus gracilior*)
Agonis flexuosa 'After Dark'
Arbutus 'Marina'
Arctostaphylos 'Howard McMinn'
Brachychiton populneus
Cedrus deodara
Cercidium ×'Desert Museum'
Cercis canadensis var. *texensis* 'Oklahoma', *C. occidentalis*
Chilopsis linearis
Cupressus sempervirens
Eriobotrya japonica
Eucalyptus caesia, *E. victrix*
Ficus carica
Garrya elliptica
Geijera parviflora
Grevillea 'Moonlight'
Lagerstroemia indica
Leptospermum laevigatum
Lophostemon confertus
Mariosousa willardiana
Olea europaea
Pinus pinea
Pistacia chinensis
Platanus racemosa
Prosopis glandulosa
Punica granatum
Quercus ilex, *Q. lobata*, *Q. suber*
Ulmus parvifolia
Umbellularia californica

DO YOUR RESEARCH

Before choosing any plant for your garden, scan your neighborhood to see what species thrive, and especially notice those potentially receiving little to no care. By researching what does well in your neighborhood, you understand your microclimate better and choose plants that have a better rate of success in your area.

Also, always research the sun, water, and drainage requirements of plant material before putting them in a design. For example, *Cercidium* ×'Desert Museum' likes intense summer heat, so it is not a great option for the coastal area of Northern California. Additionally, when selecting trees or palms that are going to be located close to hardscape or foundations, always research the potential for root damage and whether it is classified as a good street tree.

In general, make it a practice to research the sun, water, and drainage requirements of any plant material before putting it in a design. For example, some of the plants listed do best when protected from winter temperatures below 30 degrees Fahrenheit here in the eastern San Francisco Bay Area, while others survive down to 20 degrees. Consider planting sensitive plants close to a house, fence, or the canopy of a tree for the best protection.

Clockwise from top left: *Cupressus sempervirens, Brachychiton populneus, Prosopis glandulosa, Quercus lobata*

Clockwise from top left: *Brahea armata, Butia odorata, Jubaea chilensis, Chamaerops humilis*

THE ACACIA AND EUCALYPTUS DEBATE

Eucalyptus and acacia get a bad rap in California. Eucalyptus trees are seen as messy, highly flammable, disease prone, invasive, and weak under strong winds. However, this genus contains quite a few manageable and smaller varieties, with many being tidy, low water, flowering, pollinator attracting, and perfectly sized for residential gardens.

Regarding acacias, many people think these plants are super allergenic, but because they are insect pollinated, their pollen doesn't easily become airborne. While some people suffer from acacia allergies, if you feel sniffly, more likely it's due to oaks, pines, or grasses—not acacias. Like the eucalyptus, there are varieties that are beautiful, fast growing, small in scale, and pollinator supporting, making them excellent candidates for many low-water gardens.

Essential Palms

Brahea armata, B. calcarea, B. clara, B. edulis, B. moorei
Butia odorata
Chamaedorea radicalis
Chamaerops humilis, C. humilis var. *argentea*
Jubaea chilensis
Sabal minor, S. 'Riverside'
Trachycarpus fortunei
Washingtonia filifera

Essential Cacti

Ruth started buying and adding cacti because she thought that her garden needed them for contrast, as a lot of her succulents sported the same one or two shapes. She believed cacti (unlike agaves and yuccas) only belonged in certain parts of RBG, but over the years these plants have come to be commonly associated with her vision. The collection of barrel, pad, columnar, and globular forms adds unique structure to a lush, dry garden, with many acting as living sculptures.

Almost all cacti feature spines, which cleverly protect them from nibbling predators, sunburn, and evaporation. They grow on stems (the paddles or columns are actually stems) that have adapted to storing large amounts of water. Cacti also have beautiful ephemeral, often iridescent, blooms in a wide array of colors ranging from clear white to yellow, orange, pink, and red. Despite only lasting a few days (and sometimes only opening at night), these flowers are showstoppers for both humans and pollinators.

Cacti can tolerate much colder temperatures if their roots remain dry and not soggy. We recommend planting cacti from March through September when the soil is warm and the plants will actively push out new roots. Be sure to mix volcanic rock into

Different varieties of cacti forms thrive in RBG.

Above: *Mammillaria geminispina* is a globular cactus.

Above right: *Ferocactus glaucescens* is a barrel cactus.

the soil (in our regional clay soils we usually recommend 70 percent volcanic rock to 30 percent native soil) and slightly mound the earth so the crown of the plant (the area where the stem meets the roots) sits at least an inch above the level ground. The first cactus Ruth planted was *Cereus hildmannianus*. Here are other common forms of cacti:

GLOBULAR

Small, round, and clumping, these are good repeated in the front of a bed, providing an interesting structural rhythm. Varieties include *Mammillaria geminispina* and *M. vetula* subsp. *gracilis*.

BARREL

This type of cactus creates a bold, round presence in a garden, adding a good dose of form to a design. Varieties include *Echinocactus grusonii*, *Ferocactus glaucescens*, and *Lobivia formosa*.

COLUMNAR

These vertical cacti act as narrow, upright focal points, leading your eye through the garden. This shape is also great alone in a container or in a line along a wall, fence, or pathway. Varieties include *Cereus hildmannianus*, *Cleistocactus strausii*, *Pachycereus marginatus*, *P. pringlei*, *Trichocereus pachanoi*, and *T. terscheckii*.

Clockwise from top right: *Cereus hildmannianus*, *Cleistocactus strausii*, *Pachycereus marginatus*

WHY PLANT CACTI?

- They are unthirsty, undemanding, and usually very low maintenance.
- Many are tolerant of extreme heat.
- Some are tall and spiny and can act as an unconventional security system when planted under a window or as a living fence.
- Cacti have a coarse, sculptural texture and form that make them a great balance for soft or wispy plants or as a focal point.

PADDLE

Ranging in size from a few feet to over ten feet tall, these are some of the easiest cacti to grow and propagate. Additionally, large paddle species can hide an unattractive fence or create a fence of their own. Varieties include *Opuntia ellisiana*, *O. ficus-indica* 'Burbank Spineless', *O. gomei* 'Old Mexico', *O. santa-rita*, and *O.* ×'Walk In Beauty' series.

Essential Aloes

Ruth's garden notably contains an abundance of different aloes, with special thanks to aloe expert Brian Kemble for adding the vast majority of them. Aloes provide coarse texture in a lush, dry garden, and while many burst into bloom in the doldrums of winter, some bloom in the other seasons as well.

Opuntia santa-rita

Aloes come in a wide variety of sizes and are easy to incorporate into many residential scale gardens. Their plump leaves provide sculptural shape, and although many aloes have toothed margins, they are quite soft. You can get the same coarse texture of an agave or cactus but without any teeth or spines. Additionally, aloes do well in cultivation. While they like sharp drainage (when water can move quickly through soil because of the presence of mineral matter), many do well in soil that has received little amending. They also thrive in pots. Regarding maintenance, Ruth maintained a "wildscaping" approach, where she left the dead leaves—or "skirt"—on her tree aloes to transform into another sculptural form. She liked the visual balance of the crown, or rosette, of fresh leaves at the top of the plant combined with the texture of the dried brown leaves encircling the trunk and how it reflected how the plant would look in nature. Others prefer the clean lines and architecture of a trimmed trunk or stem with a lush crown or rosette. Ultimately this is purely an aesthetic choice and doesn't affect the health of the plant.

Clockwise from top left: *Aloe striata*. A bed dominated by aloes at RBG, *Aloe speciosa*. *Aloe brevifolia*

OUR FAVORITE ALOES

Tall: *Aloe africana, A. arborescens, A. 'Hercules', A. marlothii, A. speciosa, Aloidendron barberae*

Medium: *Aloe cameronii, A. distans, A.* 'Hellsk-loof Bells', *A. lukeana, A. maculata, A.* 'Moon-glow', *A. nobilis, A. striata, A. wickensii*

Low growing: *Aloe* 'Blue Elf', *A. brevifolia, A. capitata, A.* 'Cynthia Giddy', *A. polyphylla, A.* 'Safari' series

Above: *Aloidendron barberae*

Right: *Aloe arborescens* (yellow flowers)

Aloes come in a variety of shapes and sizes: tall (more than three feet), like *Aloe speciosa*; medium (up to three feet), like *A. striata*; and low growing (eighteen inches or less), like *A. brevifolia*.

There are four key design elements of aloes. The first is that larger plants can act as focal points or specimens. The second is that they offer soft yet coarse texture. The third is that many bloom in the winter, bringing welcoming color and luring hummingbirds to the garden when many plants are dormant. Lastly, smaller aloes provide a wonderful "grassy" effect, like a meadow or tufts of grass when massed together.

Essential Agaves

Agaves play a crucial component in lush dry gardens, as they offer year-round interest and bold structure. An important thing to know about these plants is that they are monocarpic, which means that, once they bloom, they die. Fortunately, many of them pup, or produce offsets at their base, providing you with replacement plants in advance.

Agaves were one of Ruth's favorite plants and have always played a key role in her garden. In fact, agaves were one of the few plants she incorporated into beds throughout the garden. Many of the photos featuring Ruth in her later years feature the dramatic *Agave franzosinii*. Like Ruth, we think every garden can benefit from the addition of an agave, or two, or more. These plants add bold texture and a wide variety of leaf color, and are very low maintenance. Agaves range in size from under one foot to ten feet tall, so there is truly one for any size garden. And with their rosette shape, they provide sculptural interest to the garden.

The iconic and stately *Agave franzosinii* with *Penstemon spectabilis* at RBG

Many agaves have long terminal spines and teeth along their leaf margins (armed), while some are peacefully unarmed. Many agaves pup, while others are solitary growers. Pupping can be nice if you want a large cluster of plants, but if you want a single specimen, then either be prepared to dig out the babies annually or select a variety that doesn't produce offshoots.

Be aware that agaves can't be pruned to fit in a space, so be sure you understand the mature size of the plant before you put it in. Nothing looks worse than an agave with half of its leaf cut off because it protruded into a path. Lastly, agaves appreciate sharp drainage, so if you don't have free-draining soil, we recommend you do some amending.

WHY PLANT AGAVES?

- They come in a variety of sculptural rosette shapes, some small and tight, other broad and arching.
- Agaves can be a wonderful addition in garden designs, especially when the large types are used as accents and the smaller ones as companion plants.
- Being evergreen, agaves can provide year-round substance to a garden bed or container while also needing minimal maintenance.
- Generally, they are deer-resistant.
- Some produce pups so you can remove and transplant these free starts or gift them to friends.

OUR FAVORITE AGAVE VARIETIES

Cl=likes to clump

Large (Six feet +): *Agave americana* (Cl), *A. americana* (variegated) (Cl), *A. americana* var. *marginata*, *A. franzosinii*, *A. weberi* (Cl)

Medium (Three to six feet): *Agave americana* var. *medio-picta* 'Alba' (Cl), *A. angustifolia* (variegated), *A. attenuata* and hybrids (Cl), *A. desmetiana* 'Variegata', *A. montana*, *A. ovatifolia*

Small (under three feet): *Agave* 'Blue Flame', *A.* 'Blue Glow', *A. bracteosa* (Cl), *A. lophantha* 'Quadricolor' (Cl), *A. macroacantha*, *A. mitis* (Cl), *A. parryi* var. *truncata* (Cl), *A. victoriae-reginae*, *A. vilmoriniana*

Clockwise from top: *Agave americana* (variegated), *Agave desmetiana* 'Variegata', *Agave weberi*

Clockwise from top left: *Agave montana*, *Agave macroacantha*, *Agave parryi* var. *truncata* (CI), *Agave* 'Blue Flame'

Essential Soft Succulents

Recently, succulents have been gaining in serious popularity. And it's easy to see why; they come in various shapes, sizes, and a wide range of colors, generally don't require a ton of water or attention, and are easy to propagate. Another great quality is that many soft succulents thrive and survive in a wide variety of climates. This laissez-faire attribute explains why you can find succulents almost everywhere—clothing stores, supermarkets, and, of course, on multiple racks at garden centers.

A succulent is any plant having water-storing tissues in its leaves, stems, or roots. The word "succulent" is a very broad term, including many plants, such as cacti, agaves, and echeverias. When talking about soft succulents, we refer to plants without spines, teeth margins, or glochids (the hairlike spines found on Cactaceae plants). Also, did you know that some soft succulents prefer all day sun on the coast but inland prefer morning sun?

WHY USE SOFT SUCCULENTS?

- They are user-friendly. When given the proper soil, water, and exposure, succulents thrive with minimal care. Many are also simple to propagate.
- Soft succulents show off vividly colored leaves, providing year-round interest.
- They grow well in garden beds, rock gardens, and containers. Some soft succulents even make great ground covers.
- When massed together, soft succulents create a bold impact. Consider *Sedum reflexum* 'Blue Spruce' or *Sempervivum arachnoideum*.

Right: Soft succulents interspersed with agaves in a crevice garden

Opposite: *Echeveria ×imbricata* and *Lotus berthelotii*

OUR FAVORITE SOFT SUCCULENTS

Aeonium arboreum 'Zwartkop', *A.* 'Sunburst', *Cotyledon orbiculata* 'Winter Red', *Crassula* 'Blue Waves', *Dudleya brittonii*, *Echeveria* 'Afterglow', *E. agavoides*, *E. elegans*, *E. gibbiflora* hybrid, *Graptopetalum paraguayense*, *Kalanchoe luciae*, *Lampranthus* 'Hot Flash', *Oscularia deltoides*, *Ruschia lineolata*, *Sedum nussbaumerianum*, *S. rupestre* 'Angelina', *S. spathulifolium* 'Cape Blanco', *Sempervivum arachnoideum*, *Senecio ficoides* 'Skyscraper', *S. serpens*

Opposite, clockwise from top: *Aeonium arboreum 'Zwartkop'* (foreground), *Echeveria agavoides* (hugging boulder), *Dudleya brittonii*

Left: *Sedum rupestre* 'Angelina' surrounding *Aloe brevifolia*

Above: *Senecio ficoides* 'Skyscraper'

Essential Shrubs

Midsize shrubs (herbaceous and woody plants) make up the backbone of any lush, dry planting design. Some are evergreen and others deciduous (meaning: lose their leaves seasonally). While some bloom throughout the year, others only occasionally set small, insignificant flowers. Being superb multitaskers, some shrubs act as both anchors to planting beds and provide a wide variety of visual interest. Be aware that some shrubs require more pruning and pampering than others. If a shrub flowers prolifically or grows fast, then it shifts itself into the higher maintenance category.

Opposite: *Leucadendron salignum* 'Winter Red' surrounded by blooming aloes at RBG

WHY USE SHRUBS?

- You need a border, hedge, or living fence.
- A flowering or architecturally bold shrub can be a focal point.
- Shrubs create the living structure of a garden.
- Shrubs soften hard edges of hardscape and built structures, such as a house, patio, fence, pergola, or arbor/trellis.
- Shrubs can act as the walls of a garden.
- Shrubs often balance other elements in a garden (like trees, focal points, and structures).
- Many are low water and low maintenance.

Try massing one type of shrub, like this *Lavandula ×allardii* 'Meerlo', for a bold yet soft effect.

A blooming *Grevillea* 'Long John' provides an eye-catching backdrop.

OUR FAVORITE SHRUBS

Tall and Screening Shrubs (six feet +): *Acca sellowiana, Adenanthos sericeus, A.* 'Silver Haze', *Afrocarpus gracilior (syn. Podocarpus gracilior), Atriplex lentiformis, Bambusa multiplex* 'Alphonse Karr', *Banksia praemorsa* (red form), *Ceanothus* 'Concha', *C. thyrsiflorus* 'Snow Flurry', *Frangula californica, Grevillea* 'Kings Fire', *G.* 'Long John', *Hakea francisiana, Leucadendron* 'Ebony', *L.* 'Safari Goldstrike', *L.* 'Wilson's Wonder', *Myrica californica, Pittosporum tenuifolium*

Clockwise from top left: *Banksia praemorsa* (red form), *Leucadendron* 'Wilson's Wonder', *Grevillea* 'Kings Fire'

Midsize Shrubs (three to six feet): *Alyogyne* 'Ruth Bancroft', *Banksia ashbyi* (dwarf form), *B. spinulosa* 'Schnapper Point', *Eriogonum giganteum*, *Euphorbia characias* 'Silver Swan', *Grevillea* 'Superb', *Leucadendron* 'Hawaii Magic', *L.* 'Jubilee Crown', *L. salignum* 'Winter Red', *Leucospermum* 'Blanche Ito', *L.* 'High Gold', *L.* 'Tango', *Olea europaea* 'Montra', *Pelargonium* 'Chocolate Mint', *P. graveolens*, *Protea cynaroides* 'Arctic Ice', *P.* 'Pink Ice', *Salvia africana-lutea*, *S. clevelandii*

Clockwise from left: *Leucospermum* 'Blanche Ito', *Euphorbia characias* 'Silver Swan', *Leucospermum* 'High Gold'

Top: *Salvia clevelandii*

Bottom: *Banksia ashbyi* (dwarf form)

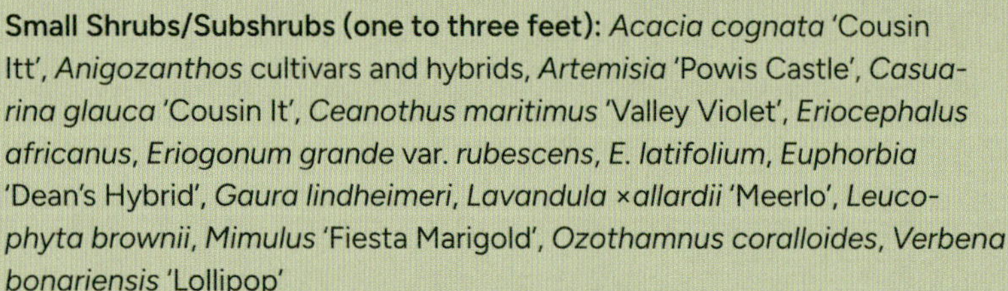

Small Shrubs/Subshrubs (one to three feet): *Acacia cognata* 'Cousin Itt', *Anigozanthos* cultivars and hybrids, *Artemisia* 'Powis Castle', *Casuarina glauca* 'Cousin It', *Ceanothus maritimus* 'Valley Violet', *Eriocephalus africanus*, *Eriogonum grande* var. *rubescens*, *E. latifolium*, *Euphorbia* 'Dean's Hybrid', *Gaura lindheimeri*, *Lavandula* ×*allardii* 'Meerlo', *Leucophyta brownii*, *Mimulus* 'Fiesta Marigold', *Ozothamnus coralloides*, *Verbena bonariensis* 'Lollipop'

Clockwise from left: *Lavandula ×allardii* 'Meerlo', *Acacia cognata* 'Cousin Itt', *Leucophyta brownii*

Eriogonum grande var. *rubescens*

Essential Ground Covers and Vines

Ground covers and vines are sometimes afterthoughts in garden designs, but they should move up the ladder of importance, as they can be key problem solvers and the crucial last step in your planting design. These multitasking plants can be a key element in your landscape, adding the finishing touch.

The unsung heroes of a garden, ground covers have an almost magical way of tying together a bed when the same variety is used throughout. Even a landscape that might err on the busy or disjointed can pull itself together and visually look more cohesive and finished when a single ground cover is used. Vines, on the other hand, can amp up the maintenance factor, as they tend to require routine tending. Generally they are fast growing, quickly providing screening and softness, which for many makes them an appealing addition.

Dorycnium hirsutum, *Aloe striata* and hybrids at RBG

WHY USE GROUND COVERS AND VINES?

- Ground covers can cover bare earth, acting as a living mulch.
- Some ground covers can control erosion and stabilize slopes.
- Vines can quickly hide an unsightly fence or view and enhance privacy.
- Ground covers and their dense blanket effect can help choke out weeds by keeping light from reaching the soil, where seed germination happens.
- Vines can create a lovely backdrop for other plants.
- Vines can break up long stretches of a fence.
- Ground covers and vines can highlight hardscapes and focal plants.
- Ground covers and vines can increase biodiversity.

The densely growing *Ceanothus thyrsiflorus* 'Diamond Heights' provides a beautiful living mulch in this composition.

A blooming pink and white *Erigeron karvinskianus* spills over the path's edge.

OUR FAVORITE GROUND COVERS

Achillea clavennae, *Achillea* 'Moonshine', *Aeonium simsii*, *Arctostaphylos* 'Emerald Carpet', *Arctotis* 'Pink Sugar', *A.* 'Pumpkin Pie', *Artemesia californica* 'Canyon Gray', *Banksia petiolaris*, *B. repens*, *Calylophus berlandieri*, *Carex tumulicola*, *Ceanothus griseus* var. *horizontalis* 'Diamond Heights', *Chrysocephalum apiculatum* 'Silver and Gold', *Dichondra argentea*, *Diplacus aurantiacus*, *Dymondia margaretae*, *Epilobium septentrionale* 'Wayne's Silver', *Erigeron karvinskianus*, *Eriogonum grande* var. *rubescens*, *Euphorbia resinifera*, *Grevillea* 'Poorinda Royal Mantle', *Hebe pimeleoides* 'Quicksilver', *Helleborus argutifolius*, *Heuchera maxima*, *Lampranthus* 'Hot Flash', *Leymus condensatus* 'Canyon Prince', *Lotus berthelotii*, *Muhlenbergia dubia*, *Myoporum parvifolium* 'Putah Creek', *Nepeta ×faassenii* 'Walker's Low', *Origanum vulgare* 'Aureum', Oscularia deltoides, *Pelargonium sidoides*, *Plectranthus neochilus*, *Ribes viburnifolium*, *Rosmarinus officinalis* var. *prostratus*, *Salvia* 'Bee's Bliss', *Sempervivum arachnoideum*, *Senecio mandraliscae*, *Stachys byzantina*, *Teucrium cossonii*, *Tradescantia pallida*, *Verbena lilacina* 'De La Mina', *V. lilacina* 'Paseo Rancho'

Clockwise from top left: *Banksia petiolaris, Dymondia margaretae, Heuchera maxima, Aeonium simsii*

Opposite, clockwise from top left: *Pelargonium sidoides, Lotus berthelotii, Stachys byzantina*

Left: *Grevillea* 'Poorinda Royal Mantle'

OUR FAVORITE VINES

Bougainvillea 'Barbara Karst', *Clematis ligusticifolia*, *Ficus pumila*, *Hardenbergia violacea*, *H. violacea* 'White Out', *Kennedia nigricans*, *Passiflora edulis* 'Frederick', P. 'Snow Queen', *Tecomaria capensis*, *Vitis* 'Roger's Red', *Wisteria frutescens* 'Amethyst Falls'

Clockwise from top left: *Clematis ligusticifolia*, *Kennedia nigricans*, *Passiflora* 'Snow Queen'

Essential Proteaceae

If you are familiar with this family of plants, then you know how visually captivating Proteaceae plants are, especially when they put on a flower show and gift you with floral material to create bouquets and flower arrangements. Adding to this, Proteaceae plants are evergreen and can skillfully act as year-round powerhouses, working well as foundation plants, especially when massed together or when used as focal features. (Oh, and bonus, nibbly deer tend to leave them alone.)

Thanks to Troy McGregor, owner of the design-build company Gondwana Flora, a plethora of Proteaceae plants successfully joined the Ruth Bancroft Garden. In fact, Troy reintroduced a variety of climate-appropriate and low-water South African and Australian shrubs, succulents, and waterwise trees. Ruth tried growing these plant families years ago, but they perished due to little knowledge existing at the time in the US about their soil and fertilizer requirements.

The bulk of Proteaceae plants are native to Australia and South Africa, and come in an assortment of sizes and colors, making these unthirsty plants proof that dryness can also be uniquely attractive. In general, they are easy to take care of but do require different care than other plants and have very specific requirements to survive and thrive.

A variety of *Leucospermum* blooming at the Ruth Bancroft Garden

TROY'S TOP TIPS FOR BUYING, PLANTING, AND MAINTAINING PROTEACEAE PLANTS

- Buy smaller plants, as they are less expensive, establish quicker, and are less likely to be root-bound. One gallon is preferable. Proteaceae have very sensitive roots. If it is root-bound, very, very lightly tease apart the roots when planting.
- The best time to plant is either fall or spring.
- Proper drainage is key to these plants' success. If you have poor drainage, berm up the soil twelve to eighteen inches high, and allow for slump and compaction. For existing gardens, mix in pumice or red lava. Do not use bags of planting mix, as they are full of water-retaining wood products. For containers, choose a large pot with two to three large drain holes and use drywall tape across the holes (no broken pots or rocks).
- Plant them high and water thoroughly.
- Place a pet rock on the south side of the plant to protect the roots and collect heat during the day and release it at night.
- These plants are very light feeders and originate from sandy soil that is gritty, low in phosphorus, and nutrient deficient. If you choose to fertilize, use liquid seaweed and steer clear of fish fertilizer due to the strong smell.
- Use iron chelate to correct chlorotic leaf yellowing.
- Tip prune regularly during the early years to create a fuller and healthier plant. For *Leucadendron*, prune mid- to late spring.
- Harvest the flowers like a florist, meaning cut long stems (making sure to leave foliage on the stem below the cut), remove the foliage from the lower part of the cut stem before placing in water, regularly cut a half-inch off the bottom, and frequently change the vase water.

WHY IS MY PROTEACEAE DYING?

Symptoms of phosphorus toxicity include shoots dying, leaves browning and then dropping off, then inevitable death. Unfortunately, there is no cure. A more common culprit of rapid death is root rot and poor drainage.

OUR FAVORITE PROTEACEAE PLANTS

Well-known genera in this family include *Adenanthos*, *Banksia*, *Dryandra*, *Grevillea*, *Hakea*, *Isopogon*, *Leucadendron*, *Leucospermum*, *Protea*, and *Telopea*. The following list is based on Troy's firsthand experience in relation to the East Bay's Mediterranean climate. Some of these plants may not do well in your region, so a little research is recommended: *Banksia blechnifolia*, *B. integrifolia*, *B. praemorsa* (yellow form), *Grevillea* hybrid 'Peaches and Cream', *G.* 'Superb', *Hakea petiolaris*, *Leucospermum* 'Brandi Dela Cruz', *L. reflexum*, *Protea cynaroides* 'Mini King', and *P.* 'Pink Ice'

Below: *Banksia heliantha*

Opposite, clockwise from top left: *Hakea petiolaris*, *Banksia blechnifolia*, *Protea cynaroides* 'Mini King', *Banksia praemorsa* (yellow form)

Essential Focal Point Plants

Ever wonder why some gardens immediately catch your attention and draw you in, while others appear jumbled and disorienting? When too many elements stand out, our eyes refuse to settle and focus on just one thing, and we ultimately feel visually overwhelmed. This is where focal point plants can work wonders and save the day, shifting our gaze and telling our eyes what to notice first so that we can move on to the rest of the garden's story. Like any big design statement, they should be used sparingly. A focal point plant is a strong, dramatic specimen with bold leaves, an arresting architectural shape, or an oversized stature. These plants call attention to themselves. Also, most focal plants are evergreen or have a lengthy season of interest. With skillful and strategic pruning and training, you can sometimes turn a common plant into a focal plant.

Yuccas, palms, and *Dasylirion* draw your eyes into the garden.

WHY USE FOCAL POINT PLANTS?

- They draw and direct the eye through the garden or to a specific area.
- They anchor a planting composition to provide a sense of weight.
- Just a few—or even one—focal point plants can set the tone for the entire design.
- They can create a visual starting point and/or an exclamation point in a garden.
- Multiple focal points can act like visual stepping stones when repeated through a garden.

Below: A blue-leaved cycad glows in the understory at RBG.

Right: A dramatic composition near the RBG entrance gate

Above left: *Yucca rostrata,* Above right: *Yucca gloriosa* 'Bright Star'

Opposite: *Cycas revoluta*

OUR FAVORITE FOCAL POINT PLANTS

Agave americana var. *medio-picta* 'Dwarf Alba', *A. franzosinii, A. weberi, Aloe marlothii, A. plicatilis, A. speciosa, Aloidendron barberae, Chamaerops humilis, Cleistocactus strausii, Cycas revoluta, Dasylirion longissimum, D. wheeleri, Dioon edule, Echinocactus grusonii, Encephalartos horridus, Euphorbia ammak, Jubaea chilensis, Opuntia robusta, O. santa-rita, Pachycereus marginatus, Strelitzia reginae, Xanthorrhoea preissii, X. quadrangulata, Yucca gloriosa* 'Bright Star', *Y. linearifolia, Y. rostrata*

Essential Dry Shade Plants

Admittedly, dry shade is one of the hardest spots in a garden to design. Areas less frequented by warming rays exist in many gardens yet, we still want to fill these places with pretty plants. We often think of shade as wet environments, but in summer dry climates you will often find dry shade.

There are three types of shade. Dappled shade is when small amounts of light filter through trees for most of the day. High shade is when the shade comes from a high tree canopy or building far above the ground and ambient light reaches the area. Deep shade is when no direct sunlight reaches the area, creating dark spaces. A deep shade dry garden is the trickiest of all gardens.

Although it's tempting to immediately go out and buy plants because you love them, first notice how the sun moves across the sky and affects the light quality in your space throughout the day and through the changing seasons. Take notes, make lists, research your proposed plant's likes and dislikes. You don't want to put a sun-loving plant in the deep shade.

Opposite: Eucalyptus trees provide high, dappled shade in The Garden.

Below: A variety of palms shade Ruth's pond.

OUR FAVORITE DRY SHADE PLANTS

While we love helpful plant lists just like you do, we also especially love plants that can work well in both those slightly shady spots as well as sunny situations. Look for (S/S) below, meaning these plants do well in both sun and shade. Always research the sun, water, and drainage requirements of plant material before putting it in a design. For example, some of the plants listed are low water if grown in the shade but medium water if grown in full sun here in the inland San Francisco Bay Area.

Essential Succulents for Dry Shade: *Aeonium canariensis* (and hybrids), *A. simsii*, A. undulatum, *Agave angustifolia* 'Marginata' (S/S), *A. attenuata*, *A.* 'Blue Flame' (S/S), *A. bracteosa* (S/S), *A. mitis* hybrids (S/S), *A. vilmoriniana* (S/S), *A. weberi* (S/S), Aloe maculata (S/S), *Beaucarnea recurvata* (S/S), *Beschorneria albiflora* (S/S), *B. yuccoides* 'Flamingo Glow', (S/S), *Bulbine latifolia* (S/S), *Cleistocactus strausii* (S/S), *Crassula* 'Blue Waves' (S/S), *C. tetragona* (S/S), *Dasylirion longissimum* (S/S), *Echeveria agavoides* (S/S), *E. elegans*, *Echeveria ×imbricata* , *Gasteria aci-nacifolia × Graptoveria* 'Fred Ives' (S/S), *Haworthia* spp., *Manfreda undulata*, *Mangave* spp. (S/S), *Nolina nelsonii* (S/S), *N. palmeri* (S/S), *Sedum spathulifolium* 'Cape Blanco', *Sempervivum arach-noideum* (S/S), *Tradescantia pallida* 'Purple Heart' (S/S), *Yucca filamentosa* (S/S),*Y. gloriosa* 'Bright Star'(S/S), *Y. pallida* (S/S)

Below left: *Agave angustifolia* 'Marginata'; Below right: *Beaucarnea recurvata*

Clockwise from top left: *Nolina nelsonii, Beschorneria albiflora, Agave bracteosa, Echeveria ×imbricata*

Essential Woody and Herbaceous Plants for Dry Shade: *Abutilon palmeri* (S/S), *A.* 'Tiger Eye', *Acanthus mollis* (S/S), *Aquilegia shockleyi*, *Arthropodium cirratum*, *Billbergia nutans*, *Carex divulsa* (S/S), *Ceanothus* cultivars (S/S), *Chondropetalum tectorum*, *Cordyline australis* 'Torbay Dazzler', *C. fruticosa* 'Soledad Purple', *Correa* 'Ivory Bells', *C. pulchella* 'Pink Eyre', *Daphne odora*, *Dianella revoluta* 'Little Rev', *Eriogonum crocatum* (S/S), *Fatsia japonica*, *Fremontodendron* 'San Gabriel' (S/S), *Hebe pimeleoides* 'Quicksilver', *Helleborus argutifolius*, *Heuchera* cultivars and hybrids (e.g., 'Canyon Delight,' 'Obsidian,' and 'Ginger Ale'), *H. maxima*, *Iris unguicularis*, *Lomandra* 'Arctic Frost' (S/S), *L. confertifolia* 'Del Sol', *L.* 'Platinum Beauty' (S/S), *Mahonia eurybracteata* 'Soft Caress' (S/S), *Mimulus* 'Jelly Bean Dark Pink', *Osmanthus* ×*fortunei* 'San Jose' (S/S), *Philodendron* 'Xanadu', *Plectranthus argentatus*, *Ribes viburnifolium*, *Russelia equisetiformis*, *Salvia spathacea* (S/S)

Below left: *Chondropetalum tectorum*; Below right: *Mimulus* 'Jelly Bean Dark Pink'

Opposite top: *Eriogonum crocatum*; Opposite bottom: *Lomandra* 'Platinum Beauty'

Left: Fernlike *Mahonia eurybracteata* 'Soft Caress'

Above: Flowering *Correa* 'Ivory Bells'

Opposite: Trailing *Russelia equisetiformis*

Essential Power Player Plants

Are you searching for plants that can multitask and do well in difficult situations? Look no further than power player plants. These plants thrive despite extreme heat, lack of water, and occasional freezing winter temperatures. Some of these candidates also make great solutions for that notoriously tricky area between the sidewalk and the curb, aka "the hell-strip," while others on this list can tough it out through reflective heat.

Blooming *Cereus hildmannianus* at RBG

A grassy swath of *Muhlenbergia rigens* at the top of the stairs

POWER PLAYER PLANT KEY

- Reflective Heat (RH): The heat generated by the wall of a building or a fence that is south or west facing (in the northern hemisphere).
- Extreme Temperatures (ET): Can take extreme dry heat as well as freezing temperatures.
- "Hellstrip" Plants (HP): A median "hellstrip" planting can have three difficult factors to contend with: reflective heat from the surrounding pavement, potentially no irrigation, and car and foot traffic. Plants in this category should be able to thrive regardless of these factors.

Our Favorite Power Player Succulents: *Agave bracteosa* (HP), *Aloe marlothii* (RH), *Hesperaloe* cultivars (ET), *Opuntia* ×'Walk in Beauty' series (ET)

Our Favorite Power Player Trees: *Cercidium* ×'Desert Museum' (ET), *Cercis occidentalis* (HP), *Chilopsis linearis* (ET)

Our Favorite Shrubs and Herbaceous Plants: *Banksia integrifolia* (RH), *Clarkia purpurea* (HP), *Eschscholzia californica* (HP), *Hakea francisiana* (RH), *Lomandra* 'Lime Tuff' (HP), *Muhlenbergia rigens* (HP), *Romneya coulteri* (RH), *Salvia apiana* (ET), *S. clevelandii* hybrid/cultivar (RH), *Sphaeralcea* cv. (RH)

Opposite, clockwise from top left: *Hesper-aloe parviflora* 'Desert Dusk', *Salvia clevelandii* hybrid/cultivar, *Romneya coulteri*

Left: *Sphaeralcea* cv.

CHAPTER

· 4 ·

Lush Dry Gardening in Containers and Small Spaces

Container gardening is defined as plants growing in a pot or other vessel as a single specimen or a group of plants. The beauty of growing in containers is that you don't need a ton of space to create an attractive garden. Container gardening also grants you the opportunity to try your hand with low-water plants, like Proteaceae plants or succulents, before potentially graduating to in-ground planting or a larger space.

Containers work well in the transitional spaces between garden beds and built elements, so consider adding them by doors and gates, along paths, at the edge of a patio, or next to a grouping of furniture. It creates a sense of place and wayfaring and allows you to compose small, interesting plant vignettes. The only downside is that containers often need more care than plants in the ground because they don't benefit from the soil, water, and exposure of a garden bed.

Page 136: You can create living "flower" arrangements or miniature gardens like Troy McGregor did with this composition.

You can create living "flower" arrangements or miniature gardens.

REASONS TO CREATE A LOW-WATER CONTAINER GARDEN

- You have limited space, inside or outside.
- Containers filled with plants can soften a space or add another design element.
- Plants can be added to an area with little or no planting beds, like decks, patios, or balconies, or to areas where the soil is poor or contaminated.
- By planting in containers, you can move your garden around or take it with you, if the pot or container isn't massively heavy. This is especially helpful for those who rent and want to take their plants with them when they move.
- Filled containers make unique gifts for friends and family.
- You can completely control the soil that plants live in and tailor the mix to fit the plant's needs.
- By raising up plants, you bend over less during installation and maintenance, which is a total back saver and brings the plants to eye level.
- Elevated containers keep plants safe from rambunctious pets and kids.
- One large beautiful pot can hold court alone.

Tips for Creating a Lush, Dry Container Garden

An assortment of well-chosen pots creates a welcoming entry in a garden by Karly Silicani.

When planting just one container or creating an entire container family, think about each one like a mini-ecosystem where the factors of light, heat, soil, and moisture come into play. Also, remember to apply some of the basics of design when grouping containers: scale, proportion, and repetition. When flowers aren't the major star in your containers, emphasize contrasting leaf textures and shapes.

Start with a design theme before choosing plants. By choosing a consistent style of container, the grouping will feel harmonious. The container style should reflect that of the garden in general but also speak to one another visually. For the plant matter, if you are using cacti, mix in other succulents or woody/herbaceous plants that have the same feel, be it desert, contemporary, or a hybrid. The same could be said for a California cottage garden, where you might mix salvias, penstemon, and wax myrtle for a soft and floriferous look.

Choose your container wisely. Not all containers are suitable for every exposure and every plant. Look for a container in a size able to accommodate the plant with room to grow. In general, go up one pot size from the nursery pot, as soil in containers can retain excess water and cause root rot. Also, porous pot materials—like terra-cotta—absorb moisture, circulate air better, and don't retain heat as easily due to their thickness. However, plants living in terra-cotta may require more frequent watering. Glazed ceramics can be pricier and don't offer the same level of cooling or evaporative benefits, but they do gift the garden color and a reflective element.

Consider how the container relates to the other elements in the garden. Should it be bold or blend in? Do you want to direct the eye to something in the distance or have it rest in a particular place?

Remember proper drainage. If your container is missing drain holes, drill a few. The water needs to drain out, or the plants will rot. And avoid putting things in the bottom of your pots such as pottery shards, rocks, or plastic water bottles. This will cause a perched water table and slow the drainage, promoting rot in the plant's roots. If you are concerned about the soil clogging the drain hole, cover it with Sheetrock tape or a piece of mesh netting before adding the soil.

Choose the correct soil. The soil blends you use in the ground (bedding blends) are not suitable for containers (which should be a potting mix). Furthermore, with containers it's important to match the right soil mix to your specific plant. Remember that these are mini-ecosystems. Some plants may want soil that holds more water or has more nutrients, while others may require leaner or faster draining mixes. Understanding the nutrient and drainage requirements of the plant and using the appropriate soil are just as important with containers as with plants in the ground. Every couple of years consider changing out the soil in your containers, if possible.

Top-dress your container. By adding a top layer of mulch (usually decorative gravel), your composition will look more finished. Mulch also holds the soil down when the plant is watered, keeping it from spilling over the edge. Additionally, like in the ground, the mulch protects the soil from the elements, helping it retain moisture and stay cool. When planting, make sure to leave about an inch of room at the top of the container so you can lay in the mulch.

For easier watering, group plants with similar water needs. And remember that plants in containers only have access to the nutrients you feed them. In order to keep them productive and attractive, learn what food is needed and feed accordingly. Good natural fertilizer choices include fish emulsion, compost tea, and seaweed extract.

Below left: Containers allow for plantings in tight spaces like the corner of a house, shown here in Walker Young's garden.

Below right: The bright color of this trio of pots complements the plantings in Julia Holland's garden.

CONTAINER IDEAS

The Single Specimen: Choose one bold plant per pot that flaunts a strong architectural shape to maximize drama.

The Single Pot: Add one large pot to an area and either plant a specimen plant or a collection of plants (a container garden).

The Mix-It-Up: Add a variety of differently shaped pots to an area to create a pleasing composition with some heft.

Above: A simply designed pot can command a more diverse planting, but a highly decorative pot looks better and less busy with a solo specimen or a clumping rosette. Consider: *Aeonium*, *Echeveria*, and *Sempervivum*.

Left: Using the same color and shape brings cohesion to a grouping of potted plants.

DON'T REUSE GROWER SOIL

Avoid reusing grower soil because it has been formulated for fast growth, frequent fertilization, and the specific water regime of the grower. It's not designed for long-term plant growth. When planting up your container garden, gently knock off old soil (being careful of the roots) and then replant in fresh soil.

A good rule of thumb when selecting plants for container gardens is to think about a thriller, a spiller, and a filler.

OUR FAVORITE PLANTS FOR CONTAINER GARDENS

The Thrillers: *Beaucarnea recurvata, Chondropetalum tectorum, Crassula tetragona, Senecio ficoides* 'Mount Everest'

The Fillers: *Delosperma* 'Fire Spinner', *Echeveria* ×*imbricata, Gasteria acinacifolia* × *Graptoveria* 'Fred Ives', *Heuchera* 'Lemon Chiffon'

The Spillers: *Dichondra argentea, Kalanchoe fedtschenkoi, Russelia equisetiformis, Senecio peregrinus, Tradescantia pallida*

Left: The swollen trunk of the *Cyphostemma juttae* creates an interesting container specimen in Max Cannon's garden.

Above: A jubilant collection of succulents creates a colorful combination in Molly Stone's garden.

Tricks for Gardening in Small Spaces

Are the words "yard" and "landscape" too generous to describe your garden? No worries, because a small space shouldn't deter you from creating a big impact. Whether you have a tiny front yard, a slim side yard, or a pocketbook backyard, with the right plants, design tricks, and ideas, you can transform any space into a useful low-water, visually successful garden.

A limbed up *Acacia pendula* provides room for a colorful collection of *Mangave* and other succulents in this small front yard.

TOP DESIGN TIPS FOR A SMALL GARDEN

- Start by defining what you want the garden to do. Once the purpose is decided, then you can organize the space and find plants to suit your needs. Is the garden a sitting area or passageway? Do you see it out of a window or only when you enter it? These types of questions will really help you make the most of your design.
- Break up the area into smaller rooms with the purpose to create the illusion of more space. Yes, this totally sounds counterintuitive, but this trick works. Use existing features like walls and fences as well as plant matter to create the "walls" around a sitting area. Have pathways meander or zigzag through the space to break up the flow, and then tuck seating areas off to the side. Just like you don't want to put all your furniture against your walls, bring your planting beds into the middle of your space to create enclosure, screening/hide-and-reveal, and visual interest.
- Go up! Use vertical elements such as an arbor, a vine-covered trellis, or an espaliered tree to make use of vertical space. Also consider plants with slim profiles, like columnar cacti or a yucca that forms a trunk. Focus on plants that grow up, not out.
- Be bold. Now is the time to add some seriously dramatic plants. Creating that strong visual interest in the foreground distracts your eye from the confines of the space.
- Layer color and texture. To gain more space to underplant and create layers, trim the lower branches of trees and then plant at their feet, making the most of all the space you have.
- Create immediate interest by focusing on foliage over flowers. Also, factor in colorful foliage for year-round appeal.
- Repetition of plants creates a cohesive space. Even picking one plant and repeating it makes the composition feel bigger and more pulled together.

The repetition of bold rosettes makes this small garden feel larger.

- Obscure the horizon/change the path so the end goal is hidden. This fools the eye into thinking the space is bigger, even if it ends right around the corner.
- Place a mirror at the end of a path, on a fence, or on the side of a building. This reflects the garden back at you, giving the appearance of it continuing beyond and visually doubling the space.
- Build or buy raised beds for added height and interest, creating a more dynamic, multilayered design.
- Remember that cool-colored plants (blue, green, and purple) when placed at the back of a space add visual depth. Warm-hued flowers and foliage (red, yellow, and orange) placed toward the middle and front bring the space closer to the viewer.
- Like color, textures play with the eye. Finely textured plants recede in a space and can make it look bigger when placed at the back of a planting area. Coarse or bold foliage placed in the foreground or midground can create immediate interest but can also dominate a space, so use them judiciously.
- Look for plants described as "dwarf" or "compact." These will take up less space in a small garden.
- Use plants that can multitask. Choose those that factor in more than one of these considerations. *Cordyline australis* 'Torbay Dazzler' is a great option for a plant that has a vertical growth habit and a lot of visual interest in the color of the leaves. Showy echeverias are great to plant in masses in the front of beds because they are easy to repeat and have nice coarse texture and year-round color in their leaves.

Above: These aloes and aeoniums were carefully selected for their small mature size.

Opposite: The soft foliage of the grasses mixed with the coarse foliage of the agaves creates year-round visual interest.

TOP PLANTS FOR SMALL SPACES

Below is a list of our go-to plants for small spaces. You can use this as a plug-and-play guide to fill in your own small space. Just remember to mix the colors and textures of the leaves and flowers for the most dynamic visual interest.

Vertical Element: *Acacia vestita*, *Agonis flexuosa*, *Callistemon* 'Cane's Hybrid', *Cleistocactus strausii*, *Cordyline australis* 'Torbay Dazzler', *C.* 'Red Star', *Ficus pumila*, *Trichocereus pachanoi*, *Yucca elephantipes*, *Y. rostrata*

Below left: *Callistemon* 'Cane's Hybrid'

Below right: *Yucca rostrata*

An *Agonis flexuosa* tree provides a welcoming canopy in this curbside garden.

Medium-sized, Bold Texture: *Agave* 'Mateo', *A. mitis*, *A. parryi* var. *truncata*, *A. pygmaea* 'Dragon Toes', *Echinocactus grusonii*, *Philodendron* 'Xanadu', *Protea cynaroides* 'Mini King'

High Impact, Low Profile: *Aeonium simsii*, *A.* 'Sunburst', *Banksia blechnifolia*, *Ceanothus griseus* var. *horizontalis* 'Diamond Heights', *Eriogonum arborescens*, *Lampranthus* 'Hot Flash', *Mangave* 'Lavender Lady', *Oscularia deltoides*, *Sedum nussbaumerianum*, *Sempervivum* 'Gold Nugget'

Clockwise from left: *Oscularia deltoides*, *Eriogonum arborescens*, *Mangave* 'Lavender Lady'

Opposite: *Aeonium* 'Sunburst'

CHAPTER

5

Laying the Foundation for a Resilient Garden

While many think of plants when they hear the word "garden," the infrastructure is what truly holds the design together. Laying the proper foundation upon which you build your garden is the most important thing for long-term success. And while it may feel fussy and expensive spending money on things you may or may not see, in the long run you will save money and time and generate better results.

A designer can be a helpful guide for you in the decision-making process for phasing (installing your garden in stages over time), if it works within your budget. We often get asked by clients about this. Many people think it gets them what they want without spending all the money upfront because they can budget and do the work over time. Phasing the installation of your garden can be implemented, but there are some key factors to be aware of. The easiest way to phase a project is to do one section at a time, i.e., first the front yard and then the backyard or vice versa. But even if you are installing only one part of your garden at a time, you'll still need to consider laying the foundation for the next phase when it comes to demolition, electrical, gas, water, drainage, and hardscape so you don't have to disrupt your completed work.

In the following sections, we briefly discuss the nonplant material aspects of the garden installation process. Each one of these topics is an entire field of study of which we are only skimming the surface, but our hope is to give you a basic understanding to encourage you to delve deeper into the aspects that interest or benefit you.

Soil Basics

Healthy soil truly is the foundation of any happy plant and is especially important for the long-term success of climate-resilient gardens. Like many of the topics discussed in this book, the exploration of soil in low-water gardens could fill its own tome. When starting a garden, it's crucial to understand what type of soil you have and what the soil preferences or requirements are for the plant palette you wish to use. Remember, a garden is resilient if it can withstand weather fluctuations and still thrive. One of the keys to a garden having this strength (and being lower maintenance in the process) is for the soil to be appropriate for the plant palette and vice versa.

Page 152: *Opuntia gomei* 'Old Mexico'

The two main things you should be aware of in your soil are type and nutrients. You or your landscape contractor can perform any number of tests (both simple home or complex

For many succulents to thrive in our inland climate, sharp drainage is critical.

lab) to find out your soil type and nutrient levels. With this information, you can amend your soil and select a plant palette suited to your climatic conditions.

Popular wisdom is that native plants will automatically do well in your soil simply because they are native. However, the native range of a plant can be quite limited. Understanding the plant's requirements for both soil type and nutrient balance allows you to make the most informed decision when coming up with your plant palette. All the plants listed in this book do well in our area when we amend the clay with volcanic rock (lava or pumice). We recommend you mix volcanic rock into your existing soil at a 50/50 ratio, digging down to at least twelve to eighteen inches when planting. Conversely, many would do equally well in coastal San Diego sand with some compost mixed into the soil (or nothing at all). The key is to remember that soil is one of the most important factors in the success of plants. It's easy to make assumptions, which is all the more reason to test your soil.

RBG was in a state of decline when garden manager Walker Young joined the staff in 2011. Poor soil health ran rampant, which was apparent in the dwindling vitality of the plants. As Ruth got older, RBG began to suffer from increased deferred maintenance. With his expertise and knowledge, Walker has revitalized the plant collection over the past decade, in part by addressing the soil. The following is his advice on cultivating a healthy soil biome when working with clay soil like that at RBG.

CLAY SOIL: DIGGING DEEPER

by Walker Young, RBG Garden Manager

When churning native soil high in clay, better results are achieved with a focus on structural versus nutritional amendment. Other than their particle sizes, everything else about clay soil is usually excellent, such as great structural stability and nutrient density. Clay soil contains everything to make most plants happy except sufficient ability to allow the passage of air and water through the matrix. Thus, we can deduce that maximum gains will be produced by the addition of extremely porous rock like pumice or scoria.

Organics should be applied at the surface, with best results coming from finer and more frequent applications rather than heavy smearings of material. Once the fine layers begin to infiltrate and disappear at the soil's surface, it's time to broadcast again. By introducing organics in the same manner as nature does, albeit with much more concentrated inputs, we are able to keep our microbes happy, and our gardens growing well over time.

While many tests can be done to help understand a course of action regarding soil amendment, these are usually not helpful places to start for home gardeners. Why is that? Conventional "soil tests" or "soil analysis" consist of an evaluation of the nutrient profile of your soil based on a number of samples taken from the area to be cultivated. The lens through which these results are analyzed is one of commercial agriculture, wherein massive amounts of nutrients are supplied to ensure large yields from fast-growing, energy-intensive plants.

Unfortunately, the corrections recommended will reflect an interest in short-term yield rather than long-term performance and sustainability. Moreover, they will have zero concern for the soil's microbiome—the healthy function of which is what ultimately makes nutrients available to plants—regardless of the quantities of specific nutrients present in the soil matrix.

The bottom line is that no investment in your garden pays off more over time than a thorough improvement of its soil structure. Building a drought-tolerant garden without concern for soil structure is like building a house without a solid foundation. Sure, you may get away with it for a while, but eventually something detrimental happens and it'll be a lot more expensive and difficult to jack the house up and reinforce it than it would have been to pour some solid forms at the beginning of the construction process.

With that said, here are some methods to consider:

DIG IN

Percolation tests involve digging a hole in the ground, filling it with water, and then observing how long it takes to drain. Conventional wisdom tells you that if a twelve-inch hole drains in an hour or two, you probably have adequate drainage. Unfortunately, that is inadequate drainage for most succulents and drought-tolerant plants, particularly when faced with the simultaneously cold and wet conditions of our Mediterranean winters. For best performance, we want to see pooling water drain in minutes, not hours.

ROCK OUT

We recommend using a porous volcanic rock like pumice or lava rock (scoria) as your main structural amendment over all other available aggregates because of their ability to provide permanent porosity throughout the root zone. This ensures drainage in the winter, insulation from heat waves in the summer, and, most of all, conditions that will tip the balance of power permanently toward aerobic, positive microorganisms in the soil.

Opposite: Kipp McMichael's mounded crevice garden

A MOUNDING CONCERN

Those of us not blessed with unusually desirable native soil conditions, such as the decomposed granite hillsides of northern San Diego County, need to decide between the more labor-intensive but long-term rewarding route of structurally amending our native soils with porous volcanic rock, or the less labor-intensive but potentially long-term growth limiting route of building mounds of structurally stable bedding mix on top of the native soil. Building mounds of a predominately mineral mix is also an option if you're gardening around significant mature trees that you wish to preserve.

THE WIDE VIEW

So you want to work with what you have, and you're ready to roll your sleeves up and get digging. But how? First focus on digging wider, rather than deeper. Then begin adding lava rock or pumice to the native soil like flour in a baking mix—little by little, until you have created a homogeneous mix to the desired elevation. Composts, meals, humic acids, biochar, worm castings, gypsum, and other helpful amendments can then be incrementally broadcast over the mounds to augment growth and maintain healthy topsoil over time. If you're particularly eager to supercharge growth, a judicious amount of these amendments can be mixed into the matrix one time and one time only. In a large area absent of root systems from mature trees, a mini-excavator makes light work of what would otherwise be a significant amount of physical labor with shovels.

Finally, there is no such thing as too much soil structure for our plant palette, and you can always add more organics on the surface over time, but you can't go back and re-amend for better structure without ripping out your garden.

WALKER'S ABSOLUTE SOIL NO-NO'S

Avoid mixing undecomposed wood products into the soil matrix. Wood decomposition inside the matrix robs the soil of nitrogen and other essential nutrients, and often results in hydrophobic (water-repelling) soil behavior after the wood breaks down to dust.

Avoid manures of all kinds. Herbivorous animals are high-level bioaccumulators, and manure frequently contains alarming levels of all kinds of things we don't want to introduce into our gardens like heavy metals and herbicide residues. For the same reasons, avoid bone- and blood meals.

Avoid all salt-based petrochemical fertilizers. These types of fertilizers cumulatively degrade soil microbes. You'll get away with hosing the yard down with harsh chemical fertilizers for a while, and you may even make some people jealous with how ridiculously you can bloat some specimens on plant meth, but it will eventually catch up with you and there will be a reckoning. We've seen it again and again in gardens where caretakers relied on chemical fertilizers—things stop growing, strange mineral deficiencies show up, soil testing shows plenty of nutrients exist but nobody can figure out what has suddenly gone wrong. The issue is that eventually the microbiome has worn down so much that it can no longer reliably process nutrients into the bioavailable molecular forms plants need. If you already have a big stash of conventional fertilizer, stop using it in the garden and save it for your containers, where it's unlikely that there is much microbial diversity or function anyway.

Opposite: Healthy soil lays the foundation for a flourishing garden.

Above left: Walker Young's mounded front garden in Piedmont

Above right: A natural rock outcropping in Molly Stone's Berkeley garden

WHY CREATE MOUNDS?

- They add topographical interest to a flat property and create variety in the terrain.
- Mounding soil lets visitors view the garden areas from different angles.
- Mounding allowed Ruth to create contained collections, small vignettes, and concentrated areas for focusing on a color or genus. For the homeowner, mounds can make a space less daunting and more manageable.
- Mounds make staging plants more interesting, as the plants are elevated and less plant material is hidden.

Mounding in the Garden

The Ruth Bancroft Garden sits in the most unlikely place for a waterwise garden—the slope is flat, with persistent clay soil. And unfortunately, Ruth learned this the hard way when her first round of plants promptly died due to root rot and improper drainage. However, to mitigate the heavy clay, Ruth created mounds with fast-draining soil high in mineral content to rise above the inhospitable soil. For any garden facing clay soil or other poorly draining conditions, mounds can be one viable solution.

To create mounds, bring in new soil and make mounds reaching a minimum of twelve to eighteen inches high to allow for slump and settling. Avoid making steep mounds or the water will run off too quickly (and they look silly). Be sure that whatever soil you use contains a high mineral (volcanic rock, horticultural sand) content and is appropriate for your chosen plant palette. Be very aware of the manure, compost, or fertilizer potentially added, because some low-water plants are light feeders and/or sensitive to certain elements or pH levels.

WHY USE BOULDERS AND ROCKS?

- Large boulders add drama, contrast, and year-round solid texture.
- Rocks add a coarse texture.
- Boulders add visual weight and give form to a space.
- Both boulders and rocks help retain soil and add structure, especially on mounds.
- Rocks increase drainage.
- Boulders and rocks offer favorable growing conditions for certain plants such as *Eriogonum*, and make plants look naturalistic.
- Boulders with a flat side become a seat or bench.
- Boulders with a dip or impression become birdbaths when filled with water.

Boulders provide naturalistic seating in the children's nook at RBG.

Boulders

Looking for a substantial (and heavy) enhancement to your garden? Consider adding boulders. This element goes hand in hand with creating mounds, as boulders can provide both needed structure to the soil as well as naturalistic topographic interest. Boulders also work well in flat sites, adding natural focal points that need zero care and won't die. Adding to this, boulders blend seamlessly into a climate-appropriate garden, mingling well with plants that originate from inorganic gravelly soil, crumbly screes, and sharp cliffs. If your property already contains rock material, then by all means use what you have. Don't have space for boulders? Smaller rocks and gravel can also serve multiple purposes.

Think about boulders in relation to your design. Always add them *before* planting, as it's easier to plant around them after they're situated and you don't want to crush your plants or damage your new hardscape in the process. Carefully select the most attractive side or face of the boulder, then partially bury it into the soil, about one-third, leaving only a portion exposed so it looks settled in place and not awkwardly plopped down. This is an art not a science. Look at how nature places them, not as if they rolled off the back of a truck and slammed down. Artfully nestle plants next to boulders for a naturalistic look, and you can also use them for casual seating within a garden setting.

Irrigation Basics

Irrigation systems can seem complex and confusing, what with all those boxes, pipes, tubes, timers, and valves. But almost all gardens require irrigation to become established, and watering with a hose consumes excess time and water. Installing an irrigation system is the most efficient way to control your water and how it reaches your plants. This greatly impacts the health of your garden and your pocketbook while also conserving precious resources.

Ruth preferred using a sprinkler system. "I just can't see myself handling drip. Every time you put in a plant you've got to do something with that darned little hose." She was also concerned that drip would clog up with RBG's hard water.

WHY INSTALL AN IRRIGATION SYSTEM?

Irrigation systems provide water to new plantings because all new plants, even very low-water ones and even in smaller sized gardens, need consistent water to become established. By helping them establish deep roots, you help plants become resilient quicker. An irrigation system aids in the long-term success of your garden. Even after the plants have become established, there will be winters with less than normal rainfall or summers

Above left: Even low-water plants benefit from occasional summer watering.

Above right: Combining plants with similar water requirements simplifies irrigation.

of particularly punishing heat. Having an irrigation system in place allows your plants to survive through hard times.

Routine irrigation helps mitigate the risk of fire. Many hydrated plants don't catch fire, or they will burn slower than water-stressed ones; this is increasingly important during fire season and the increase of extreme heat across our region (and the world). Also, many regional and local water districts have resources and rebates to help with irrigation upgrades and lawn-to-garden conversions. It's worth doing some research to see what's available in your area.

IRRIGATION SYSTEMS

Every gardener waters their own way based on experience, system preferences, plant selections, and financial constraints. Our two favorite ways of delivering water in our summer dry gardens are in-line drip and low-flow rotors.

In-Line Drip is when the emitters are built into the tubing, usually half-inch polyethylene. This type is good for new gardens and flat spaces. It can be laid out in a grid or in a curving pattern, depending on the plant layout and if it is a new or partially existing garden. Extra bonus: with in-line drip you eliminate patching or poking new holes when you add plants, which weakens the system. Downside: it uses an excess of plastic material and may clog.

Low-Flow Rotors These are traditional-looking sprinklers that pop up from the ground when they go on. They are good for hillsides, meadows, and established gardens. There are many new low-flow spray options currently available that can apply almost the same amount of water as drip. Extra bonus: rotors use less plastic material and don't tend to clog. Downsides: you may have to run the low-flow types for longer to get adequate saturation, plus, as plants mature, they might block the spray from reaching their plant neighbors.

Grevillea petrophiloides 'Big Bird'

HYDROZONING

Hydrozoning is when you place plants with similar soil, sun, and water needs together. By doing this thorough advance planning, you reduce water use while also protecting certain plants from being over- or underwatered. Factors determining different zones can include exposure, water pressure, existing plants, and the new plant palette. This environmentally friendly way of designing a garden can be segmented into four zones:

Regular irrigation. In a waterwise garden, this would be your food production, either vegetable beds or fruit trees.

Reduced irrigation. Often used for establishing trees or keeping mature specimens healthy in times of extreme heat or drought.

Limited irrigation. This area receives occasional supplemental water. This is the most common category in low-water gardens.

Zero irrigation. This area receives no supplemental water, only natural rainfall. Very few gardens fit in this category and most of those will have long seasons of dormancy.

IRRIGATION BEST PRACTICES FOR ESTABLISHMENT

New plantings require regular water for the first two to three years to develop a deep, healthy root system. In an inland, summer dry climate, you'll need to water for thirty to forty-five minutes three

> **WATERING CACTI AND AGAVES**
>
> Because cacti and agaves originate from regions with summer monsoons, they grow quicker when watered deeply by hand in the hottest months of the summer, up to two to three times a week. Let the ground dry out between watering.

times a week in the summer months, depending on the types of plants and flow rate of the irrigation system. Watering at night reduces water evaporation and most plants enjoy night drinking.

When trying to determine the amount and frequency of irrigation schedules for either a new or existing garden, it's good to pay attention to the daytime temperatures and the soil moisture. Low-water plants prefer to dry out between waterings, and many prefer to receive deep soakings. Overwatering a plant can kill it just as much as underwatering, however; if you notice leaves curling or drooping/flagging, this often means your plant needs a good drink. Install a smart controller, as it will skip the run cycle if it unexpectedly rains, and you can make adjustments from your phone.

In the spring, always check your irrigation system. Start by flushing out your system to remove buildup and particles, then move on to looking for breaks or unknown leaks. Lastly, make sure all the emitters are properly flowing and not clogged.

The Power of Mulch

Ah, mulch. It's like the fancy icing on the cake. It's amazing how mulch can really pull a garden, or even a container, together. A layer of mulch says, "Ta dah! I am finished ... for now." But that isn't its only positive attribute. Mulch is one of gardening's oldest techniques to protect the roots of plants from cold, heat, and/or drought as well as to encourage healthy mycorrhizal (fungal) activity in the soil.

Mulch covers up exposed soil to lessen evaporation of water from the upper layer. With mulch, soil doesn't dry out as quickly and more water is available to the plants. Mulch reduces weed seed germination by blocking the sun when used thickly. Mulch also makes it easier to pull out the weeds that do grow.

Mulch creates a clean, finished look, and can hide and protect unsightly irrigation tubing. It moderates the soil and air temperature, creating a more hospitable microclimate for the plants, and it increases root growth by providing protection from the sun and rain. Tired of soil splashing on plants? Mulch prevents this as well. Wood mulches decompose slowly and release small amounts of nutrients into the soil, and they encourage fungal, insect, and earthworm activity, which in turn aids in soil health.

CONSIDER THESE MULCH OPTIONS

Gravel mulch comes in a wide variety of colors, shapes (sharp or round), and sizes. For most gardens we recommend ⅜ inch, but sometimes we mix in larger pieces in the same color for more visual interest. Our favorites are: French Country (also sold as Nursery Crush, Yosemite Crush, and others) and California Gold. A good rule of thumb is one inch thick throughout the garden bed. Never use decomposed granite (DG) as a mulch or mix it into the soil. The particles are too small and compact and smother the soil. If you like the visual look, use California Gold ⅜ or something similar.

Wood mulch falls into two categories: processed and unprocessed. Processed wood mulch has a cleaner look and you can determine how much you want to get based on your need. Try to steer clear of artificially dyed mulches. We like to use undyed natural mulch because it turns a beautiful gray over time. If you want mulch with color, choose those that have been dyed with vegetable dyes.

You can get unprocessed wood mulch for free from tree trimming companies. Usually, you must get an entire truckload, the pieces vary widely in size, and often leaves and sticks

Gravel is great for succulent gardens and for those wanting a very tidy look. Gravel mulch is easy to hand weed and stays in place when you use an electric leaf blower.

Wood mulch is great for a wide variety of gardens. If you have deciduous trees and use wood mulch, leave the leaves on the ground when they fall into your beds and your soil will get an additional layer of protection and nutrition.

are mixed in. This mulch is usually freshly cut and therefore should dry out and age (cure) for a few months before putting it in your garden beds. Unprocessed wood mulch is a good option if you are sheet mulching a lawn or have a large unmanicured area where you want to control the weeds. Ask the tree company what wood makes up the mulch, as you want to avoid some trees, such as walnut or camphor, because of natural chemicals that can prevent other plants from growing when in contact with it.

Don't worry that free wood mulch contains bugs or pathogens. This is something that comes up with the use of salvaged raw materials, but rest assured, most insects can't survive the chipping process, and by letting the mulch cure, the pile heats up and potentially destroys any pathogens or diseases.

Wood mulch should be applied one to two inches thick in most of your garden beds and be kept at least six inches away from your house to keep insects from wandering in and excess moisture building up. Plan on replacing and refreshing this material every two years.

MULCH TIP

Keep a ring clear of mulch (gravel or wood) at the base of a plant for airflow. Aim for two inches. Also, don't dig wood mulch into the soil if you add plants because this will introduce harmful bacteria, and when the mulch breaks down it depletes iron supplies and causes leaf yellowing.

Weed Cloth Many people ask for weed cloth as part of their garden installation. While the inclination is understandable, it should never be used. Weed cloth inhibits water and oxygen from reaching the soil and getting to the roots of plants. Also, earthworms and many beneficial insects living in the soil die due to a reduced amount of oxygen. Weed cloth also doesn't prevent weeds, as many common garden weeds are spread by seeds through the air. Additionally, it's a petroleum product and not biodegradable. The same goes for black plastic mulch. If you really want to smother potential weeds coming up through the soil (like Bermuda grass), use cardboard, either clean boxes or rolls from the hardware store. This material will block out the light to the weeds but also break down over time and feed the soil.

Hardscape

The term "hardscape" broadly refers to built elements in a design, such as patios, retaining walls, paths, and decks. Essentially, any element in the design that is constructed is considered part of the hardscape on the landscape plan, as opposed to the softscape, which are the plants. Hardscape is the most expensive part of the design process both in materials and labor. It's also important to remember that many of the materials used in hardscaping are not biodegradable, unlike plants. This means that once built elements have been made and placed in our gardens, they are going to exist on the planet for much longer than we will. While we strongly encourage you to experiment with different plants in your garden, we also encourage you to think carefully about your hardscape. Be judicious in your selections and try to use recycled materials when possible.

HARDSCAPE MATERIALS

Depending on what is being built, a multitude of possible materials exist. For example, pergolas can be built out of wood or metal. Retaining walls can be wood, stone, concrete, metal, or CMU (concrete masonry unit). For the purposes of this book, here are the materials we use often for patios and paths, since these features are in most garden designs.

Brick works in a variety of garden styles. Its appearance varies depending on the color of the brick and the pattern in which it is laid. Installation is labor intensive and best done by professionals. For casual paths and patios, we recommend laying brick in sand versus mortar to allow water to percolate back into the aquifer.

Concrete is a versatile material to use in the garden. It can be poured to any size or shape, from large driveways to small, board-formed pads. Concrete can also be tinted in a vast array of colors and finished from smooth to rough. Pebbles can be added to the surface to create a natural aggregate surface. Concrete should always be installed by a professional. The labor required depends on the application, and it's always crucial to consider drainage when using concrete.

Decomposed Granite often called DG, is a fine quarried material that is highly porous, comparatively inexpensive, and fairly easy to install (though it does need to be done correctly for even compaction). When using DG, add edging to create the borders. We recommend steel edging, not plastic, because even though it costs a little more upfront, it lasts much longer and is recyclable. DG should not be placed directly next to doors, as it can stick to feet and shoes and scratch floors. DG can be installed as a DIY project, but care must be taken with the process.

Consider a smooth, continuous surface for primary paths.

Gravel is a great economical material for paths and patios, and not only comes in a wide variety of colors but works with any garden style. Like DG, gravel allows water to stay on-site, which is important for groundwater replenishing, and it requires some form of edging to be properly contained and to prevent scattering. Gravel does not require professional installation but works best when the site is properly prepared.

Pavers This term is generally used to refer to paving blocks. They come in a wide variety of styles, colors, sizes, porosity, and price. Have pavers installed by a professional and expect a moderate labor cost. Paver options exist for any style of garden, and we recommend selecting classic patterns to support the longevity of the design.

Poured-in-place concrete gives a modern look to this garden by Terramoto.

CHOOSING YOUR HARDSCAPE MATERIAL

Utility: Think about how the space is used. If it's a heavily used path or patio, or the area needs to be smooth for wheelchairs or walkers, you should seriously consider concrete or pavers. If it's a narrow path on the side of your house, DG might be the best option. Also, different materials affect the speed you can move across them. For example, a pea gravel path can slow the walking pace down, whereas a wood boardwalk allows you to move quickly through the space.

Style: Different materials convey different looks. Some, like gravel, are fairly versatile, while others, like wood or concrete, can be quite specific style wise. Knowing the general style of your garden helps narrow down the appropriate hardscape choices.

Budget: A key factor determining hardscape choices is cost. Hardscape is the most expensive part of a project, so being creative in this area is an effective tool in your value engineering toolbox.

Existing hardscape: By using what already exists, you can save time and money, and create less waste. However, remember to integrate existing with new, a process you can begin by using what you have as a visual stepping off point when selecting new hardscape. In general, you don't want to have more than three different hardscape materials in a space, as this will cause it to look disjointed and hodgepodge. If you keep existing hardscape elements, like brick or stone, then match and repeat them in the new design. This will blend the old and the new and create cohesion.

Natural Stone is an excellent hardscape material due to its versatility and longevity. Depending on the application, it can be installed by either a professional (complex design, stone cuts) or a homeowner (pre-cut pieces set in gravel). If set in sand or gravel, stone allows for percolation.

Tile is often used to create a seamless inside/outside flow. Tile comes in a wide range of styles and price points, which makes it a good choice for all garden styles. Because it is most often set on concrete, tile isn't permeable, and needs to be installed by a professional.

Wood is commonly used for raised and at-grade decks. It's also beautiful when used for pathways or "boardwalks." Both applications can be costly, depending on the type of wood and application. Wood for stair treads can, however, be an economical choice. It's always better to use real wood versus a manufactured wood-looking material because authentic wood is biodegradable and renewable.

Bioswales and Rain Gardens

With any garden design, consider the movement of water on the site, primarily in terms of percolation and drainage. Due to increased drought and poor water management for both agricultural and nonagricultural purposes, groundwater levels are decreasing, so it's more important than ever to keep the water that comes to your garden, either from rain or irrigation, on-site. If space and budget allow, add a bioswale or a rain garden. These engineered spaces are designed and graded so runoff naturally drains to them and then filters into the earth. You can also funnel the downspouts from your house into them. Many people think about capturing rainwater to water their plants, but it's just as important, and a lot easier, to send this water back into the depleted aquifer.

Drainage of water in any landscape project is also critical and even more so now due to erratic weather patterns. Be sure you understand how water moves through the site, paying close attention to areas that routinely pool up or remain waterlogged, and then invest in a proper drainage system, such as French drains, if necessary. These drains can move the water to your bioswale or rain garden (if you have them), taking the water from a place where it can do damage to a place where it can do good.

Also consider percolation and permeability when making your hardscape choices. Many hardscape materials, including many pavers, do not allow water to move through them and you will need to incorporate drainage in your project when you use them. It's a great practice to use as much permeable hardscape as possible.

Path lights directed down illuminate a walkway while minimizing light pollution.

Lighting

Many people want to incorporate landscape lighting in their garden designs, and while we understand the beauty in a well-lit landscape, there are other factors to consider. For example, landscape lighting is highly disruptive to the animals and insects that frequent (and support) your garden at night. Excessive light has also been shown to disturb the migratory patterns of birds. Many communities, in fact, have instituted dark sky ordinances to combat this type of harmful light pollution. If you do choose to add lighting to your garden, please consider these suggestions:

- Use lights rated DarkSky compliant. These lights minimize glare and direct the light down instead of polluting the night sky.
- In situations where uplighting is wanted to highlight certain plants, be intentional and judicious where you place uplights, washes, and in-ground well lights.
- Do not put your lights on a timer. Instead, use a manual switch to turn them on and off. That way you are only illuminating your garden when you are home to enjoy it.

In lieu of a traditional lawn, the *Acacia cognata* 'Cousin Itt' and *Aloe* 'Hercules' give this garden an interesting and modern look in this garden by Troy McGregor.

Life Not Lawn

In our current confusing climate, we need to redefine what "curb appeal" looks like. Homeowners no longer need to default to clipped boxwoods and thirsty turf. Manicured lawns demand copious amounts of water, fertilizer, and toxic weed control, as well as the constant labor of mowing and edging. All those unhealthy factors combine to create a biodiversity desert and resource-guzzling zone, and contribute to an unsustainable environment. Replacing lawns with waterwise, climate-appropriate plants can pay off for both the homeowners and the environment. Where a lawn exists, we strongly suggest removing it and instead creating a productive, healthy, and vibrant space.

Lawns can be removed in one of two ways: sheet mulching or manual removal. While many believe that sheet mulching is the only way to preserve soil health, avoids dump fees, and is an easy DIY project, having someone come in and dig out the grass will be just as beneficial in the long run.

SHEET MULCHING

Sheet mulching is a very popular grass removal strategy for small lawn-to-garden conversions. Most people can complete the process without help from a professional; with some elbow grease and resourcefulness you can spend very little to no money.

Karly Silicani put together this combination of California natives and flowering low-water plants from other regions to create habitat where a lifeless lawn once existed.

Sheet Mulching in Ten Steps

1. Continue watering your lawn, even if it is only once a week, through the summer.
2. Come fall, dig a two-inch-wide by one-inch-deep strip between the grass and any hardscape.
3. Cut the grass as low as you can. Leave the clippings.
4. Put down a layer of compost one to two inches deep on the grass. This step is optional.
5. Put down a layer of cardboard over the grass. Make sure the cardboard pieces overlap by at least an inch and that the entire lawn, including the edges, is covered. (You can either buy rolls of cardboard at the hardware store or use recycled cardboard boxes—just make sure to remove all labels, tape, or metal staples. Bike or appliance stores usually have leftover thick boxes perfect for sheet mulching.)
6. Cover the cardboard with two to three inches of mulch, preferably undyed wood chips. You can buy wood chips or get some from a local tree service.
7. Leave this mulch lasagna in place for six months and let the rain and elements do their thing. If you have to tackle this process in the dry season, it's important to thoroughly water the area with a hose at least once a week because water is key to the decomposition process.

8. Once the six months have passed, sweep the mulch away from where you want to plant, cut a hole in the cardboard with a small handsaw (if the cardboard hasn't completely broken down already), dig a hole, and plant away.
9. Once you've planted, lay irrigation and cover everything back up with mulch.
10. Hand-pull any inevitable grass sprouts popping through.

Presto! Bye-bye, lawn, hello garden.

MANUAL REMOVAL

Removing your lawn manually is a good option if you want to put in your garden right away or you are building mounds. It takes a lot of strength and muscle to dig out grass, so for some, this process might require hiring professionals. Remember that the dug-up grass can be disposed of or used as a base for your mounds as long as you put at least twelve to eighteen inches of soil on top.

With a pickaxe or a small ride-on tractor with a shovel attachment, go to town on the grass but try to remove as little of the soil as possible. If you are creating a traditional flat garden bed, amend the soil with the appropriate amendment (compost, volcanic rock, etc.) and then plant. If mounding the area, aim for a minimum of height of twelve to eighteen inches with a balanced soil blend appropriate to your plant requirements.

Most grasses benefit from being cut back once a year in the late winter season.

A Word on Maintenance

Even low-maintenance gardens need some level of attention. Why? Because plants and gardens are growing, living things, not stagnant furniture. Gardening is also more about the journey and should be seen as a continual work in progress. Many low-water gardens exist that only require quarterly or biannual maintenance. It's important to keep this in mind when you start the garden design process. If you like to work in the garden or have a good maintenance gardener, then feel free to fill your garden with plants requiring lots of pruning. But if you want to minimize maintenance, be sure to choose plants demanding less fuss. The bottom line is that, over time, the more consistent care and observation a garden receives, the healthier and more beautiful it will be.

Block out time to work on your garden; if you can't commit to a regular schedule, then hire professionals to come on a regular basis.

It's frightening and disappointing how quickly a good garden can go bad without proper maintenance. Remember that your garden is an investment that you spent money on, so you should make sure you protect it from crashing.

Ask questions. Observing your garden is critical, but so is trying to figure out why certain things happen or haven't happened, so that the same mistakes don't recur. Some questions to ask: Why did that plant die? Why did ants invade? Why is that plant getting so long and leggy? Why is it not blooming? Many gardeners, both beginner and experienced, have anxiety and guilt around losing plants. Even those who have been gardening a long time don't know the reasons for every failure. But with observation and experimentation (like Ruth!) you can learn over time.

Think about potential garden problems. What can go haywire? A lot. Soil, moisture, drainage, disease, weeds, pests, deer/gophers, and temperature can easily cause havoc in the garden. It is critical to pay attention and address issues early on before they get the upper hand. Remember that we are working with the garden, not against it; when we realize that we are collaborating with nature and with the specific conditions, habits, and needs of plants, we can make better choices to solve inevitable problems.

See a few weeds? Don't turn your back and hope they magically disappear. They won't. Weeds are opportunistic and not only do they affect the appearance of your garden, they also enjoy stealing important nutrients and moisture from the soil at the expense of your chosen plants. One trick is to pull weeds while they are young and haven't set seed. Another is to weed right after a light rain so the soil releases the roots easier. If you hand weed regularly after a garden is first installed, you'll notice a large decrease in weeds after the first year or two.

THE FIVE TOP GARDENING MISTAKES TO AVOID

1. Overfertilizing or applying the wrong fertilizer. Too much plant food, especially a high-nitrogen fertilizer, can encourage lush growth that attracts aphids, mites, and whiteflies. Another issue is applying damaging fertilizers high in phosphorus to plants in the Proteaceae family.
2. Ignoring weeds and letting them go to seed.
3. Placing plants too close together so they are crowded from the start.
4. Purchasing plants that are root-bound or overgrown in their pots. Overgrown plants with congested roots are already stressed, likely to have root issues, and may struggle to get established once planted.
5. Using toxic fertilizers or harmful weed and pest control products in the garden.

OUR FAVORITE TOOLS

Properly taking care of plants, and your hands, requires the proper tools. You wouldn't use a flathead screwdriver to hammer in a nail, just like you wouldn't use craft scissors to prune a bush. This is a standard list of tools, but most gardeners have their favorites for certain tasks. Side note: it pays to spend a little more on quality tools and take care of them.

- Bypass pruners
- Pruner holster
- Fish bone/scale remover
- Hori hori knife
- Handsaw with a 10- to 12-inch razor-sharp blade, in a sheath
- Loppers with a 3- to 4-inch blade
- Long-reach, telescoping pruners
- Tongs
- Tweezers
- Hemostat
- Narrow shovel with a point
- Gardening gloves
- Electric blower
- Box cutter

A selection of tools used in a dry garden

PART

• 2 •

Gardens Inspired by the Ruth Bancroft Garden

Ruth didn't set out to create a garden for other people or to set an example. She grew plants to learn about them and learn from them, for her to grow as a perennial student. She was deeply curious, and planted small plants even though she knew some grew glacially slow. By planting four-inch or one-gallon containers, she could watch her plants mature from baby sizes to adults. Ruth didn't have a guidebook showing her how to successfully grow low-water plants. In fact, some of the plants she put in her garden had never been cultivated before, including *Nolina matapensis*, *N. hibernica*, and *Aloe sabaea*, to name a few. Ruth defaulted and relied on good ole trial and error—a sometimes expensive and heartbreaking process.

We are the lucky ones. We have RBG to stand as our living classroom and laboratory teaching us what can thrive in the area, a leafy museum highlighting how gargantuan some of these plants can grow. Ruth's garden also visually helps us see how to combine a variety of plants, how to weave and wind them together into a pleasing scene, how to contrast shapes and textures, bounce colors around, and ultimately create a dynamic garden that is well suited to the regional environment.

Here you will visit gardens created by professional designers and enthusiastic home gardeners who have been and continue to be inspired by Ruth and her garden. And to be clear, a garden inspired by Ruth doesn't only mean copying plant choices or duplicating plant vignettes. It also means adopting some of the design principles (unity, repetition, and balance) or enlisting mounds and boulders to add height, weight, and texture and to hopefully mitigate soggy clay soil. It means gardening with resilience in mind.

To be inspired by Ruth and her garden can also manifest in ways words can't describe. The influences struggle to be labeled or pinned or captioned. Perhaps a gardener simply embraces the same desire to watch and learn and experiment. To love plants so much that it almost hurts. Inspiration comes in many forms. Different elements strike different chords with different people. Perhaps your own garden holds some of these "Ruthian" influences. And if not, maybe after reading this book it will. We sure hope so.

Page 179: *Agave franzosinii* and *Yucca rostrata*, two plant species Ruth loved, stand proud at the entrance to RBG.

Opposite: Walker Young's personal garden. Like Young, the people featured in this section are all inspired by the architecture and resilience of the Ruth Bancroft Garden plant palette.

Taking Risks for Big Rewards

LANDSCAPE DESIGNER: Kelly Kilpatrick of Floradora

LANDSCAPE CONTRACTOR: Michael-Carlos Gomez of Gomez Gardening

HOME OF: Eric and Cindy Elia, Oakland, California • USDA ZONE: 10

Sometimes you just know what you are destined to do, become, and create. Growing up in Austin, Texas, Kelly Kilpatrick was curious about plants from a young age, so deeply that she drew her first garden layout plan at eleven years old. (She still has the plan.) And similarly to what she currently incorporates into her design practice, Kelly's juvenile but budding garden plan combined edibles and waterwise ornamentals. "Jalapeños for my dad and salvias for my mom."

After moving to California, Kelly remembers one of her first visits to RBG back in the 1990s when she was studying horticulture. "Being at RBG was eye-opening and it exposed me to a variety of dry garden specimens. So many shapes, forms, and new plants to learn about." During her visit, Kelly became acquainted with some of her now-favorite plants: *Aloe marlothii*, *Eriogonum giganteum*, and *Xanthorrhoea*.

Opposite: Large boulders help anchor the garden beds and provide a nice contrast to *Senecio mandraliscae*, *Agave attenuata*, and a young *Olea europaea* 'Swan Hill'.

Below: Kelly sits in the garden.

From 2003 to 2010, Kelly jumped into all things plant related while working at Annie's Annuals & Perennials in Richmond, starting as the cuttings propagator and eventually becoming the operations nursery manager, a position in which she oversaw the outdoor crews, crop health, and weekly availability lists. "Oh, and I wrote lots of descriptive signs, which was always fun, and did a lot of plant photography for the website and catalog." Eventually it was time for Kelly to move on, so she cemented her desire to become a garden designer and work with unusual plants.

Kelly eventually acquired her own garden, which had a hideous lawn that she immediately let die and then removed. Eagerly she added all sorts of plants she wanted to experiment with. However, in a neighborhood filled with verdant weed-free lawns, her neighbors thought of her as a bit crazy. Luckily though, as her garden grew, so did local interest. "Whenever I was working in the garden, I had neighbors stop by to talk and ask questions. Inevitably I would pass on a cutting of this or a clump of that." Kelly returns to that area sometimes and notices that there are just as many planted front yards as lawns. "It's nice to see people's attitudes changing."

Curving, mounded beds provide a gentle contrast to the dramatic angles of the house.

When Kelly designs a client's garden, she usually installs around 25 to 50 percent new-to-her plants. "I don't want to keep planting the same plants over and over when there are so many new ones to try." A self-confirmed plant bachelorette, Kelly sometimes creates an entire garden around a new plant that she really wants to experiment with. "I suppose it can be a bit of a risk trying a lot of new plants at a time but with good garden sense and a little bit of research it usually pays off." Kelly also believes in pushing boundaries with the plants she is already comfortable with, like giving certain plants a little bit less water and seeing if they will still be okay.

Drifts of repeating plants in the main garden as well as the sidewalk strip combine to visually expand the garden. This allows those walking by to feel like they're strolling through the garden. *Lomandra* 'Platinum Beauty', *Baccharis pilularis* 'Pigeon Point', *Westringia fruticosa* 'Grey Box', and *Anigozanthos* 'Big Red' wind and weave together.

The front yard at her Golden Gate project was initially a sloped, weedy lawn with an excess of overgrown sheared hedges, which she immediately removed. "One problem with the garden that needed solving was the triangular layout of the lot and the house and garden [being] exposed to a long section of a busy street. We also needed to create some level areas to make the garden more usable." To remedy these issues and concerns, Kelly borrowed ideas from RBG and constructed a low stone retaining wall that meandered and curved across the front of the garden. This wall allowed the creation of a level gathering space that stepped down to a gently sloped lower planted area. The new space also provided new planting beds along the sidewalk.

"Ruth's sinuous paths and curving beds allow one to get lost in the garden, opening to new vistas at every turn. I wanted to capture that same sense of exploration and hide-and-reveal at Golden Gate." With that idea in mind, Kelly emphasized the curves of the garden and utilized the mounded soil to create privacy, hide cars, and reveal new areas. "The mounded plantings give a feeling of enclosure in the garden, like a warm hug, something that I feel at the Ruth Bancroft Garden."

Opposite: Stone benches provide secure seating and spots for appreciating the garden, and double as sculpture when not in use. The crisp angles of the stone nicely contrast with the soft plantings of low-growing *Dorycnium hirsutum*, vertical *Senecio vitalis*, mounding *Westringia fruticosa* 'Grey Box', bold *Agave attenuata*, wispy *Chondropetalum tectorum*, and blooming *Marrubium bourgaei* 'All Hallows Green'.

Drama and Texture on the California Riviera

LANDSCAPE DESIGNERS: Nahal Sohbati and Eric Arneson of Topophyla Landscape Design

LANDSCAPE CONTRACTOR AND MAINTENANCE: Steve Domines with Landlorde

HOMES OF: Gaby and Nick Swinmurn, Montecito, California; and Jovita and Alex Honor, Santa Barbara, California • USDA ZONE: both 10a

Time and time again, if a child is immersed in nature and can get their tiny hands deep in dirt, then they usually grow up into adults enamored of and enthusiastic about nature. This is true for both garden designers, Eric Arneson and Nahal Sohbati. "I became interested in plants when I would go on hikes with my father, who was a science teacher and who majored in botany," shares Eric. "He would teach me about the plants we saw in nature and the ones in our yard." After high school, Eric studied horticulture and fine art and soon became even more enthralled with plants, particularly with the tropical effect of palms.

Similarly, Nahal was raised in Iran by a nature-enthused family who nurtured her curiosity. Later on, while studying interior design in college, Nahal became captivated by the power of design and problem solving, seeing constraints as opportunities, which inevitably led her to explore biophilic design, the blending of natural solutions into design. "I realized that design is more than just a means of making spaces aesthetically pleasing but a powerful advocacy tool that can transform lives through the integration of space, analysis, and an understanding of nature." This career "aha" moment ultimately led Nahal to pursue landscape architecture.

Nahal and Eric met at the Academy of Art University in San Francisco, where they both studied landscape architecture. After graduation, they both interned and worked at various design firms before finally moving to Santa Barbara, where they started their own landscape design firm and now create site-specific, sustainable, harmonic, and meaningful outdoor spaces. Nahal explains, "As a boutique firm, we are dedicated to a process-oriented approach to design, where the client is involved in the layout, materials, and plant selection."

Opposite: An unconventional meadow bursts with a multidimensional effect, thanks to the solid olive trees, the sculptural *Brahea armata*, and the airy pink plumes of *Muhlenbergia capillaris*.

Inspiration can bubble from various sources, but RBG pioneered the way Nahal and Eric approach dry garden design in California. "One of the key lessons we learned from

Top: Gray tones run supreme in this unthirsty border filled with *Acacia iteaphylla*, striking *Agave franzosinii*, shrubby *Chrysanthemoides incana*, delicately flowered *Lessingia filaginifolia* 'Silver Carpet', and bulbous *Echinocactus grusonii*.

Above: Eric and Nahal under a magnificent *Quercus agrifolia*

Above: This inviting and casual entry garden mixes together bolder textures from aloes and agaves with an airy, grassy feel from *Leymus condensatus* 'Canyon Prince' and *Carex praegracilis*.

Ruth's work is the ability to create a diverse and textured garden while being conscious of water usage." Nahal also shares her fondness for the way RBG uses plant companionship, taking into consideration water use, growth patterns, size, and contrasting colors to create a well-layered, functional, and visually appealing garden.

"The Ruth Bancroft Garden was the first time we saw *Brahea armata*, which is now one of our favorite dry garden palms that is so perfectly adapted to California gardens. And, of course, show-stopping *Agave franzosinii*. We have installed many of these plants in our gardens with the intent to create the same dramatic effect the RBG one has, but just with added patience." Nahal and Eric make a point to add drama-filled and sculptural low-water plants, including California natives, to create bold scenes that also improve and support the wildlife habitats. "The gardening experience has taught us to redefine the concept of beauty. A beautiful garden is not static and doesn't look the same year-round. It has a life cycle, seasonal change, it's a refuge for wildlife, and is synchronized with its surrounding environment."

This thoughtful design process is evident in both Topohylla gardens. For the Ysidro garden in Montecito, Nahal and Eric were tasked with transforming a typical planting style, complete with freshly planted boxwoods, bougainvilleas, roses, etc. Luckily for them there were some excellent existing features to work with such as magnificent oaks, olive trees, and a few palms. "Where possible, we removed as much lawn as we could and replaced it with *Carex praegracilis* or other low-water alternatives to turf. Local boulders were also brought in to add more character and a sense of place to the project."

The primary guidance Nahal and Eric received from the client was to incorporate as much color as possible and to create a garden with seasonal interest and to be perfect for strolling. "They specifically wanted to see a variety of different zones with varying colors and characters, creating the feel of a botanical garden. Our aim was to craft an ambiance that stimulates the senses, inspires curiosity, and embodies the client's unique style and preferences. These different zones include African Savanna, Meadow, Cloud Garden, Shade Garden, and Oak Understory, each offering a distinct and captivating atmosphere."

For the Sycamore Canyon project, Nahal and Eric contended with a circular gravel driveway lined with lawn and tired *Pittosporum* shrubs. Fortunately, some positive plantings existed as well. "We took the parts of this yard that worked and ran with it." This included clumps of *Agave attenuata*, one mature *A. americana*, and two nice olive trees.

According to Nahal and Eric, the clients supported, and even encouraged, using low-water plants and removing underutilized lawn. The clients also appreciated bold and sculptural succulents. "With this feedback, we created a planting palette of glaucus sculptural

For a clean look, neutral-colored gravel is used as a top-dressing around *Yucca rostrata*, *Opuntia ellisiana*, *Dasylirion wheeleri*, and *Hesperoyucca whipplei*.

succulents, native ground covers and shrubs, palms, and acacias. The result to us is something that is bold, dry, yet lush."

The side play area of the property is dominated by three large existing native tree species, *Platanus racemosa*, *Quercus agrifolia*, and a large *Pinus radiata*. "These trees informed us to create a palette of plants that is completely native, well adapted to the dappled shade of these trees, and plays a supporting part of the regional ecosystem." Basically, a kid-friendly garden and a space imparting a uniquely Santa Barbara vibe.

To achieve this, Nahal and Eric dug into the visual lessons created by Ruth. "Something that Ruth did so well was integrate large sculptural plants with native or fine-leaved plants to create dramatic contrasts in texture as well as unexpected combinations." A favorite moment in the Sycamore Garden is the mix of the *Bismarckia*, acacias, agaves, and *Lessingia*. "There is a dramatic variety of leaf textures, but the color and tone hold it all together."

As landscape designers, Nahal and Eric's primary goal is to encourage a paradigm shift in what is considered beautiful, transitioning from surface-level beauty to creating an extension of the surrounding land. "We take into account the historical and current natural inhabitants of the spaces in and around our projects, and we often tell our clients that we are bringing a touch of wilderness back to their yards by incorporating native plants."

Above: Even a swath of similar tones can be interesting when different textures and shapes enter the scene, as seen in this composition of *Bismarckia nobilis*, *Acacia iteaphylla*, *Aloidendron barberae*, *Lessingia filaginifolia* 'Silver Carpet', and *Echinocactus grusonii*.

Left: A repetition of plants and space to breathe make this a welcoming and calm front entrance.

Mid-Century Minimalism

LANDSCAPE DESIGNER: Mathew McGrath of Farallon Gardens

LANDSCAPE CONTRACTOR: Farallon Gardens

HOME OF: Private owner, Oakland, California • USDA ZONE: 9b/10a

"I can recall the impression the California landscape had on me instantly," shares horticulturist and designer Mat McGrath as he tells of his journey from being an avid skateboarder hailing from Houston, Texas, to quitting high school and then jumping on a bus to San Diego. And not until years later did his horticultural interests spark. "My first experience gardening was growing cannabis indoors and the first plant I bought was a Monterey cypress." Then, at thirty years old, Mat got his first job as a maintenance gardener and apprenticed with seasoned designers. During this time he encountered agaves and aloes in addition to many other low-water, low-maintenance plants. Mat got the itch, and from this his plant obsession grew.

Opposite: Varying plant textures complement the linear cinder blocks. Shown: *Nolina nelsonii*, *Trichocereus pachanoi*, *Hesperaloe parviflora*, and *Agave* 'Blue Flame'.

Below: Mat by the cinder-block wall

Fast forward two years into his maintenance career when Mat visited RBG for one of Brian Kemble's aloe walks. Soon after, Mat met John Fairey of the famed John Fairey Garden (formerly Peckerwood Garden) during a garden design symposium at RBG. John was one of the featured speakers, and he and Mat's friendship blossomed soon after, so much so that when Mat visited his parents several times a year in Texas, John invited him to visit the John Fairey Garden if he was in town. And it was in John's garden that Mat first encountered the spectacular *Agave ovatifolia*. John had mature specimens approaching bloom size, and Mat told John, "They looked like frozen fountains."

Mat spent many days with John walking and listening as John shared his wealth of knowledge on horticulture, architecture, art, and collecting. "He also taught me to see gardens as living paintings and plants as brushstrokes." (Like RBG, the John Fairey Garden is also a preservation garden of the Garden Conservancy, and there have been horticultural exchanges between the two for years.)

Ruth, also a fellow painter of plants, met Mat at RBG, and they hit it off. Mat asked Ruth if he could ever help out, and Ruth's first

Strategic uplighting and specific spotlights enhance an architectural garden at night.

To amplify the Palm Springs feel, crushed gold ginger gravel is used as mulch.

A mid-century modern home deserves a landscape that honors its straight lines and geometric shapes.

question to him was, "What do you like to do?" Mat eventually started volunteering (the office at this point was a mobile trailer in the parking lot), and it was during that time that he began appreciating the naturalistic design elements of RBG. "What amazed me was the clustering of different species from different parts of the world but arranged according to horticultural requirements."

Mat now owns the landscape design company Farallon Gardens, and he returns to RBG each season to gather new inspiration. His design motto is "Right plant, right place," and he carefully chooses his plant palette once he gets to know a site, the way the light enters and exits the stage, the presence of pests and predators, the amount of available airflow, the soil composition. Mat adds, "And like a good long novel, RBG has seeped into my core, and I draw on this inspiration each time I put paint to canvas or plants to bare soil."

For Mat's Berkeley client, the 1958 mid-century modern house most definitely needed an updated garden, so the once dense thicket of outdated, fire-prone junipers transformed into "Palm Springs meets Oakland," per the client's request. "I wanted to come up with a simple, clean, and minimal plant palette using repetition and proper spacing so the plants could stand as living sculptures." And fortuitously, the juniper became a strange blessing because once the shrubs left, Mat discovered porous and slightly acidic soil, a quality his new plants appreciated.

Most of the bold plants Mat chose for his client's garden he had first observed at RBG, such as mature *Dasylirion longissimum*, *Nolina nelsonii*, and *Trichocereus pachanoi*. "To witness and observe fully grown plants truly helps inform which plants should be used and where plants should be placed in relation to how a garden will look over time. The Ruth Bancroft Garden has been invaluable in teaching me to think long term."

Densely Layered Horticultural Oasis

LANDSCAPE DESIGNER: Max Cannon

LANDSCAPE CONTRACTOR: Max and Justin Cannon

HOME OF: Max and Justin Cannon, Oakland, California • USDA ZONE: 10a

Opposite: Taking center stage is *Mangave* 'Aztec King' underplanted with *Lomandra confertifolia* ssp. *rubiginosa* 'Seascape' partnered with a petrified log surrounded by *Pelargonium odoratissimum* and *Mangave* 'Silver Fox' nearby. Like Ruth, Max is fond of repeating colors and textures, such as these purples and silvery blues.

Below: Justin and Max

Max Cannon, a horticulturist and plant buyer, and his husband, Justin Cannon, live in an uninspiring, garden-less neighborhood. However, the plant-devoid scene makes Max's voluptuous paradise (which is only five years young) a beacon of horticultural hope in this concrete jungle. "The backyard had widespread concrete, brick, and bark, and the front was a blank slate in a neighborhood of blank slates," shares Max. Both Max and Justin knew that they had to remove the weedy lawn in the front, so they first put cardboard down. However, this lawn removal technique wasn't kindly received. "We got a notice of violation for 'blight,' which is funny seeing as how there is a pervasive problem of illegal dumping around here."

Just like Ruth was an outlier in her lawn-filled neighborhood, Max and Justin's garden gets your attention. "I think anytime you try to do something different and visually dramatic you're going to get a lot of attention," says Max. Gradually the two transformed their garden using recycled stones leftover from construction projects, fast-growing drought-tolerant plants, and thoughtful design work, with Justin being the muscles and details guy and Max being the horticulturist and plant-obsessed partner.

Naturally, Ruth's attitude toward gardening influenced Max, in that she planted small plants not knowing whether she would live to see them mature, and how she designed plants to be beautifully layered, emphasizing foliage over flowers. Max adds, "Vignettes of bold succulents and drought-adapted perennials are a hallmark of RBG, and despite the fact that we don't have as much space as Ruth, instead of massing single types of plants as she has done, we repeat colors and textures." One such color is silver, an important hue in their garden. "We took cues from Ruth, who sprinkled it throughout her own garden. For us, silver is visually cooling and especially welcome toward the end of summer when our garden is at its driest after months of no rain."

The small patch of *Carex praegracilis* surrounding the birdbath is Max's nod to "negative space," abundant in his neighborhood, which hasn't embraced his "cramscaping" style. Shown: *Cussonia paniculata*, *Brahea nitida*, *Agave* 'Blue Flame', *Aloe tongaensis*, *Acacia iteaphylla*, Meyer lemon, and *Agave* 'Blue Glow'.

Max uses various ground covers, gravel mulches, and rocks to knit the larger plants together because, as he shares, "Bare dirt is not something we love seeing." Shown: *Brahea armata*, *Mangave* 'Aztec King', *Echium simplex*, *Pelargonium sidoides*, *Aechmea recurvata*, *Cussonia paniculata*, *Echeveria gibbiflora*, *Agave durangensis*, and *Brahea* 'Super Silver'.

For the design and overall feel, both Max and Justin agreed on indulging in "transportational gardening," the idea of a plant-filled space taking you far away. "In our garden, we have plants from all over the world. When we're out in the garden and touching these plants from Madagascar or Brazil or whatever far-flung place, I feel like I can imagine being there." Max and Justin are fortunate to garden in a climate that allows them to grow a diverse array of plants, which inevitably invites a variety of wildlife. "We have all of the usual city birds here, but we also get migratory birds like warblers, thrushes, orioles, and hummingbirds drawn in by our nectar-rich plants and water features." The garden also draws numerous native and nonnative insects, bugs, beetles, and Max's favorite: slender salamanders. "We also have a resident possum living under our staghorn fern, which is free snail control!"

Another style that Max and Justin intentionally embrace in their petite but personal garden is a bit of jumble and jamboree. "Screw minimalism and coordination!" Max

Right: The sandstone wall, made of large stone blocks left over from a work project, comprises one element in an eclectic mix of recycled materials. Max adds, "I've always wanted to live in the 'funky' house on the block and now I do!" Left to right: *Brahea armata*, *Acacia pendula*, *Mangave* 'Crazy Cowlick', *Aloe* 'Hercules', *Yucca rostrata*, and *Agave desmetiana* 'Joe Hoak'.

Opposite: *Banksia praemorsa* (red form) and the *Brahea armata* came from the Ruth Bancroft Garden. Fleshy *Aeonium nobile* rounds out the composition.

admits enthusiastically. "Being a plant buyer for a company is a dangerous job for someone addicted to acquiring plants." Apparently, Max has purchased carloads of plants after seeing them at RBG, too many to name, but he also shares that he has unintentionally killed many too. His all-time favorite from RBG is *Banksia praemorsa*, but he also became enamored with Ruth's *Aloe* 'Hercules'. "I fell in love and set off on a mission to find one!"

Max's passion for plants began from a young age, and, like many other gardeners, one of his parents introduced him to gardening. "Some of my best memories growing up are of playing in the dirt with Mom," shares Max. "My mom exposed me to the type of gardening I enjoy—the get out in the dirt and have fun type of gardener. She has always encouraged me to follow my passion for plants, even driving me around to nurseries to pick out plants before I could drive myself."

Currently, Max is in the plant subtraction phase because he spent the last years mostly adding plants because he is so taken by their beauty: the forms, colors, and fragrances. Who knows how quickly that passion will re-emerge, and he and Justin will go back to indulging in more. "I think that's the biggest lesson for me, that plants will always surprise me no matter how much I think I know. Because the more I learn about them, the more I realize there's so much more to learn."

A Beautiful Adjustment

LANDSCAPE DESIGNER: Linda McSwain and Julia Holland

LANDSCAPE CONTRACTOR: Juan Sanchez and crew

HOME OF: Julia and Colin Holland, Walnut Creek, California • USDA ZONE: 9b

Some people consider themselves fortunate to have one garden in their lifetime. Julia Holland truly hit the jackpot, as she has had three gardens in England, five in Canada, one in Seattle, and then a garden in Florida that brimmed with bromeliads, palm trees, and orchids. "I come from a British family of very keen gardeners," Julia explains. "As a child, my parents instilled in me the love for plants and flowers. My father grew prize chrysanthemums." Julia, not surprisingly, went on to become a floral designer working in London, Toronto, and Vancouver, and then co-owning a floral design company.

Opposite: A striking *Trichocereus pachanoi* showing off. Julia shares, "I like this cactus because it's very hardy and can take the intense sun. It also seems to manage our occasional frost and it blooms prolifically and often, with huge white flowers that attract multiple bees and insects."

Eventually, Julia and her husband bought a house in Walnut Creek with a generous front and back garden space—truly a large new canvas to paint/plant an English garden on. But as luck would also have it, the Ruth Bancroft Garden is very close to her home and became the first garden she visited. "I was instantly impressed and inspired by Ruth's stunningly beautiful garden and decided that in the years ahead we would make a transition from our English garden to something as close to Ruth's as possible."

Below: Julia in front of one of her favorites, *Cedrus atlantica* 'Glauca Pendula'

Julia had also realized that her sloping front garden unfortunately wasn't practical for the current changing climate and that her thirsty lawn, roses, and shrubs would have to go. "I knew I could use Ruth's expertise to make our garden somewhat similar to hers in a much, much smaller way, of course."

With the help of now-retired garden designer Linda McSwain, they tasked themselves with incorporating many plants that Julia had been growing in pots, anticipating the transition from an English garden to a climate-friendly, low-water one. Julia also borrowed many garden design ideas from RBG, such as a dry creek, large rocks, and gravel mulch. She also grouped similar colors together and incorporated different textures. "We also have a beautiful piece of rock that is a fountain. I love the sound of water in a garden."

Now Julia's corner lot garden flaunts climate-appropriate cacti, succulents, shrubs, and a stunning palo verde tree. She even has plump native *Dudleya* tucked in, which in the past she has unfortunately seen people march off with. She also fondly calls her front yard "The Impalement Garden" and says,

Her home blends seamlessly with the hardscape and provides a neutral background for colorful plants to shine. Julia shares, "Many of our plants were purchased at RBG with the help of their wonderfully knowledgeable staff."

Above left: Wispy and verdant *Cercidium* × 'Desert Museum' with bolder *Aloe ferox* underneath

Above right: In the backyard, this south-facing area gets blasted with heat but *Aloe capitata*, *Agave lophantha* 'Quadricolor', *Trichocereus* specimens, and *Euphorbia ammak* soak it all in.

"I would say that the agaves are probably my most favorite plants in the dry part of the garden—other than the fact that we're constantly impaled by these unfriendly plants. We have many agave varieties and they're constantly changing, having pups and inflorescence, which are a constant joy."

Over the years, Julia has learned not to overplant after having removed countless crowded and overgrown areas. She has also, through trial and error, learned to plant and then occasionally "cross her fingers." Julia adds, "These days you never know what the weather is going to throw at you to keep you on your toes."

Finding Joy in Experimentation

LANDSCAPE DESIGNER AND CONTRACTOR: Walker Young

HOME OF: Walker Young, Piedmont, California • USDA ZONE: 10a

Opposite: Wickedly sharp *Encephalartos horridus* hovers and stands guard over softer *Echeveria* plants.

Below: Walker with Bruce and Lola

"I suppose I've spent my entire life around drought-tolerant plants, so to a certain extent horticulture came to me by osmosis," Walker Young says. When he was young, his mom was a docent at the UC Botanical Garden in Berkeley, so he spent hours wandering through the garden while she gave tours. And even at a young age, Walker gravitated toward the New World Desert and South African collections there, but it was not until college that he took any particular interest in succulents beyond the basic familiarity he gained through exposure. "I found I really enjoyed reading in the Mildred Mathias Botanical Garden on the UCLA campus," he says, "later volunteering in the greenhouses my junior and senior years."

Then tragedy struck. At twenty-two years old, three weeks after graduating from college, Walker's mom unexpectedly passed away. To pick up some of the now loose pieces, Walker moved back home. As gardening does for many people facing trauma, working in the garden quickly became the most effective, consuming distraction from Walker's grief. He proceeded to remove sections of his mom's perfectly lovely terraced Mediterranean garden so he could plant some of the succulents he had become increasingly obsessed with. "Gardening kept my hands busy, fatigued my body, and satisfied my mind with tangible results I could touch and see. It gave me control over beautiful living things that wouldn't die unless I failed to provide for their basic needs. It provided an opportunity to obsessively research a subject I found fascinating, and to engage in a treasure hunt for spectacular objects of desire."

In 2011, after several years down this hardcore succulent rabbit hole, Walker went all out, again planting succulents and Proteaceae plants in his front yard, only to simultaneously discover that the internet and various reference books failed to answer his many questions. So began his search for a trusted local expert, who

Walker's garden beautifully blends with the style of the house. He shares, "From the fearful symmetry of an agave, to the kinetic, Dr. Seussian delight of a *Xanthorrhoea*, to the jewellike mimicry of a mesemb, drought-tolerant plants provide visual interest around the clock, whether they are flowering spectacularly or sitting completely dormant. If you learn what they want, and set them up for success, they will reward you with decades of low-maintenance, wondrous satisfaction."

turned out to be none other than Brian Kemble. The two plant-crazed people hit it off wonderfully, and so Walker started volunteering at RBG. Kismet ensued because right at that time, RBG entered its rebuilding phase, which then ultimately forged Walker into a real garden designer.

In Walker's own garden, he shares that it was, and still is, a complete experiment and a form of therapy. "I knew enough about plants to be dangerous, and my artistic eye allowed me to visualize the future well enough to get some nice plants in some pretty good positions, but I went about the construction of my garden more as an exercise in piecemeal collection rather than coherent composition." Walker claims that to an astute observer, this is

A shaggy *Aloe thraskii* accompanies *Encephalartos lehmannii* 'Kirkwood' and wispy *Xanthorrhoea preissii*.

White-tipped *Agave albopilosa*, candelabra-like *Euphorbia esculenta*, and beastly *Agave* 'Royal Spine' appreciate the full sun exposure.

still noticeable despite his sincere attempts to tie it all together with repetition, most glaringly because he admits that a visual resting point is missing. "I packed focal point plants cheek by jowl with supermodel collector items in a schizophrenic hot mess."

And despite being "an impressive pile of exotic plants," Walker is also miffed with himself for all the mistakes in his garden: not planning for maintenance access, not installing an entirely new irrigation system, not giving the eye a resting spot, not using large enough boulders to have long-term visual effect, and digging fir bark into the ground, thinking it would give his Proteaceae plants acidity but instead it robbed nitrogen from the soil and created a hydrophobic environment.

But it's not all regret. "I'm most proud of how well the cycads have done, as well as my immaculate monster *Trichocereus peruvianus*," Walker says. Over the years, many rare plants from Brian have made their way into Walker's own garden, acting as treasured gifts, and adding to the friendly reminder that both plants and people can be surprisingly and incredibly resilient.

Top: A textural vignette of *Trichocereus scopulicola*, *Aloe conifera × A. ferox*, and *Echeveria agavoides* 'Giant Red'

Bottom: A dynamic collection of substantial specimens: *Aloe sabaea*, *Agave isthmensis*, and finicky but fantastic *Phylica pubescens*

Coastal and Carefree

LANDSCAPE DESIGNER: Daniel Nolan of Daniel Nolan Design

LANDSCAPE INSTALLERS: Eric Torres and friends

HOME OF: Jeff Wright • OFFICE OF: Daniel Nolan, Moss Beach, California • USDA ZONE: 10a

Hailing from the East Coast, a substantial distance from any California dry gardens, Daniel Nolan remembers his first impressions about plants and gardening. "Growing up, our garden was wooded and relatively low maintenance with really tough plants that could survive with minimal human intervention—so no roses and lots of *Pachysandra*. I think that carries into my personal gardening style and my fondness for tougher plants."

And then there were the irises, which hold an importance for Daniel. "I was in love with irises as a child and was always begging my parents to buy different ones when we would go to the nursery, and by the time I moved away I had about a dozen different varieties in our garden." After Daniel learned that irises were also one of Ruth's intro plants to gardening, he felt a very special connection to her and that story.

Opposite: Bronzy *Yucca* 'Blue Boy' echoes the flower stalks of *Banksia praemorsa*.

Left: The simple wood boardwalk leading to the entrance perfectly reflects the coastal location. And it turns out that Jeff's son Eric and a group of his friends, along with Daniel, dug the holes and planted hundreds of plants, all in gopher baskets, then put down all the gravel/mulch. Shown: *Agave gigantensis*, *Ceanothus* 'Joyce Coulter', *Westringia fruticosa* 'Morning Light', *Salvia* 'Allen Chickering', *Acacia iteaphllya*, and *A. cultriformis*

Above: *Agave angustifolia* 'Marginata', *Xanthorrhoea preissii*, and *Westringia fruticosa* 'Morning Light' share similar tones but contrast nicely due to their different shapes. This garden, being Daniel's test plot, has gifted him with confidence in his unique plant combinations.

Right: Two *Agave gigantensis* proudly poke out of *Ceanothus* 'Joyce Coulter', while *Salvia* 'Allen Chickering' blooms with similar tones. Daniel shares, "Good garden design references the surroundings, so I selectively planted what I saw along this coast." A perfect example of this is the salvia, which smells of the sage-filled coast.

Today, however, you won't find irises in Daniel's garden designs, but you will find a collection of striking architectural plants that are carefree and make a substantial statement. He admits, "I like big masses and a lot of texture over small and fussy plants." Daniel began his career at Flora Grubb Gardens in San Francisco, diving deep into plant identification as a salesperson, which led to designing the store's displays. Within a few years, he became the in-house garden designer, working with talented architects, designers, and discerning clientele. In 2018, Daniel took his knowledge and experience and opened his own design studio, which then boosted his reputation for incorporating low-water, rare, and unusual plants into designs and for creating dry gardens that break the stereotype of being harsh and sparse.

Daniel Nolan of Daniel Nolan Design

"*Agave franzosinii* has been a staple in my work to where I won't plant straight *Agave americana* anymore because it's too common and pups too much. I owe this to Ruth's entrance planting where it's the most perfect shade of blue and chalky white, which makes for such a dramatic moment in the garden that I can't imagine trying to replicate [it] with another agave."

The other plant Daniel routinely incorporates into his designs is *Xanthorrhoea* (which is the plant silhouetted for his logo). "I first saw a *Xanthorrhoea* at Flora Grubb when two came in from a rare plant vendor and I immediately put my name on them before they could go on the floor. I hurried off to call my client, telling them they *needed* these plants for their garden." Then on Daniel's first trip to RBG, he saw *Xanthorrhoea* large enough to stand under and fell in love with them again. "I love this plant more than words can express, it's truly the most elegant and captivating plant I've ever come across. Plus, the fact that it's rare here in the US makes me love it even more." Only Daniel's favorite projects showcase these plants. "I think Ruth was a visionary for taking a chance on what must have been a few unremarkable specimens when she planted them."

Daniel's initial palette for clients featured a trove of succulents and cacti, but he has since moved on to more plants from summer dry parts of Australia, South Africa, and coastal California. "I don't like to say I use more California natives too, but I realize when you add a few into a project that it grounds the garden and gives it some needed context." This statement lives out in his studio garden, which was once the garage of his friend Jeff Wright. It's a coastal dry garden in Moss Beach that requires no regular irrigation and features repetition with some exceptional plants that offer year-round interest.

But from the start, parameters were established. Jeff told Daniel, "Do your thing but also your budget is six thousand dollars." Realizing this was a tight order, Daniel chose plants that

A spectacular blooming *Banksia speciosa*, commonly called showy banksia

would grow big and fast, but nothing larger than a fifteen gallon. (Most of the plants started as five gallons.) The exuberantly fragrant *Salvia* 'Allen Chickering' and spreading *Ceanothus* 'Joyce Coulter' thoughtfully acknowledged the native locale, and then Daniel added more exotic Australian and South African plants to create a natural but intentional garden.

"Ruth's pragmatic nature of treating her own garden like a laboratory also really influenced me in my studio garden. I planted many things that I loved but also so that I could gauge their growing habits and success rate before introducing them into clients' gardens. I think that's because at the end of the day I love plants and want to see them thrive, not suffer for fashion." Time and time again, many designers don't take risks in their plant choices because it's easier to use what's safe and familiar. But Daniel offers this: "Don't be afraid to fail. Our weather is increasingly erratic, and gardening always comes with an element of risk. It's not a personal failure if something doesn't make it, you need to learn and move on."

Native to Western Australia, *Banksia menziesii* sports serrated leaves and otherworldly autumn and winter inflorescences.

The Serial Collector

LANDSCAPE DESIGNER: Cricket Riley

LANDSCAPE CONTRACTOR: Kathleen Slattery of Gardens & Gables

HOME OF: Diane and AJ Kallet, Strawberry, California • USDA ZONE: 10a

Perched above Richardson Bay and overlooking the relatively unknown Aramburu Island sits the sloping and expertly tamed garden of AJ and Diane Kallet. Besides being a veterinarian, AJ is a self-prescribed "serial collector," meaning he cycles through stages of collecting different objects or on different themes. His garden, clearly, represents and showcases his latest obsession: dry plants.

When walking the varied stone paths, visitors are gifted with a scrumptiously layered scene and a journey that winds down the hill, around the lower edge, and then back up. Encounters of blustery areas are reminders that a body of water is near, and then as the journey winds higher, areas of calmness enter, and the coastal exposure is forgotten. It turns out that AJ walks the same way through his garden every day, sort of a meditative practice, and it's in the lower yard where he routinely sits, relaxes, and takes it all in.

Opposite: The lower gravel pathway crunches underfoot while allowing the upper garden to be appreciated from a different angle.

Below: AJ and Diane

But AJ and Diane's garden wasn't always so photogenic. Twenty-seven years ago, the horrid nongarden contained echiums and black acacias with freewheeling deer mixed in. After a few iterations, AJ realized his yard needed a total overhaul and his potted collection of large specimen plants needed a permanent in-ground home. AJ brought in Kathleen from Gardens & Gables to execute the hardscaping and create some of the walkways and terraces, then later hired Cricket from the Ruth Bancroft Garden to help make sense of his plant collection and tame the collector's chaos.

AJ discovered RBG through the San Francisco Succulent & Cactus Society and Brian Kemble. Appropriately, RBG acted as inspiration and classroom for the overall theme of his garden, in addition to the fact that AJ just loves large, sculptural, and spiky plants such as cacti and tree aloes and could see the full-grown specimens at RBG in a composed design. This firsthand experience helped AJ envision the integration of certain plants into his own garden, almost as if RBG test-drove the plants for him, coupled with the knowledgeable staff, who kept AJ from making hasty and unwise plant selections.

The lower seating area, which is the warmest (less wind) and quietest (less car noise) spot, makes the perfect place for peaceful relaxation and taking in the whole garden.

When Cricket came on the scene, she created the plant palette, helped suggest softer plants to act as counterpoints to the harsh spikes, and ultimately saved his garden from sinking into an unorganized mass of random plants. Or as AJ comments, "Cricket brought order to my disorder."

With talented help and a skilled maintenance crew, AJ's garden slowly transformed from being water intensive to less thirsty with the added relief from less regular irrigation issues. This garden morphing ensued partially because of Marin County's water restrictions. Additionally, the drought-tolerant palette is more in sync with the natural surroundings. AJ's love of large spiky specimens truly tilted the needle. And while not all of AJ and Diane's garden is drought tolerant—they kept the orchard, blueberry patch, and a handful of roses—these plants provide food and cut flowers, so their other beneficial traits override their thirst for water. "Diane likes to bring the outdoors in with cut flowers."

Aloidendron barberae holds court inside the custom fence designed after one seen at a museum in France. AJ shares, "I wanted a sculptural fence with a surface that weathered to blend into the earth tones around it and that also kept the deer out." AJ also liked the idea that you aren't just looking at a barrier but also a sweeping flow through the yard.

The rule in their garden is this: "I give every plant one chance to live. If they can't survive—with a rare exception—I will not replant another specimen of the same variety." AJ also allows plant volunteers, such as iconic California poppies, to integrate into the garden. "If they play well with others and don't become invasive, then they can stay." And as a serial collector, and with countless plant choices, AJ and the garden will continually grow, evolve, and explore new variations of what a wise and dynamic garden can be.

AJ's potting area is for summer use only. "I display my ever-evolving collection of potted succulents here. They are under 30 percent shade cloth, and most have summer flowers." In the rainy winter, AJ moves his collection to a smaller greenhouse.

Brahea clara and *Aloidendron barberae* give substance to the pathway planting, and the repetition of *Agave angustifolia* 'Marginata' on the left carries the eye through.

Dynamic and Deer Resistant

LANDSCAPE DESIGNER: Michelle Derviss of Derviss Design

LANDSCAPE CONTRACTOR: Miguel Chavez

HOME OF: Sara Henry, Novato, California • USDA ZONE: 9b

On route to a popular hiking trail in Novato sits the corner garden designed by Michelle Derviss. Originally the garden consisted of a traditional narrow brick path leading to the front door surrounded by deer-decimated roses. The new design desperately needed to take an about-face, so Michelle spent time learning about Sara's lifestyle and personal tastes and compiled a comprehensive analysis of the site. Next, Michelle began designing a garden that worked in unison with the local climate and resources, and aesthetically complemented the creativity of the client and honored her wish list.

The vision board for this garden consisted of various modern looks populated with drought-tolerant grasses and succulents. The varying colors and bold textures were a direct call-and-response to the client, who is a textile artist and graphic designer. Beyond reflecting the client, there were several other requirements: it needed to respect the house's architecture, be enclosed for the dog, incorporate two Cor-Ten steel planters, and allow the

Opposite: The gray-blue tones of the agaves, hardscape, and garage door unite the space and the elements.

Left: Trimmed olive trees punctuate the front, while flowering *Teucrium chamaedrys*, grassy *Calamagrostis foliosa*, and the iconic Ruth-inspired *Agave ovatifolia* 'Frosty Blue' add color, texture, and movement.

Left: Michelle Derviss of Derviss Design

Right: Industrial containers hold low-maintenance succulents.

southern sun to penetrate in the winter but still provide a bit of privacy. Oh, and of course the garden needed to be easy to maintain and budget friendly.

Michelle's design work routinely takes cues from Ruth and RBG. Michelle shares, "The Ruth Bancroft Garden has always inspired me to be bold with plant combinations, especially those in the agave and yucca family. Ruth was fearless in trying new plants and took chances combining dry-adapted plants. I admired her tenacity in gardening in such hot, dry, and intense sun." Michelle's interest was further piqued when she saw the mounded beds created for better drainage and the shade structure to shield some of the plants from the brutal summers.

Turns out, Novato suffers from searing hot summers like Walnut Creek. Michelle says, "I have always admired the *Agave ovatifolia* in the Ruth Bancroft Garden and I thought that would work as a bold, graphic form, plus it could be well adapted to this dry, hot site." She used this dynamic focal plant to stand out among the other dry yet colorful (and deer-resistant) plants that are laid out just like, of course, one of Sara's designed floral prints.

Silvery gray *Agave potatorum* holds its own under wispy *Chondropetalum tectorum*.

Laboratory of Love

LANDSCAPE DESIGNER: Karly Silicani of Karly Silicani Landscape Design

LANDSCAPE CONTRACTOR: Great Garden Landscaping

HOME OF: Karly and Brad Silicani, Lafayette, California • USDA ZONE: 9b

Opposite: Undemanding *Dymondia margaretae* acts as a decorative carpet in the front garden. Karly says, "When I started out, I focused more on low-water plants, but I'm increasingly focused on plants that can handle our water cycle and hold out during those tough summer months. Ideally, I'm going somewhere between two to four weeks between irrigation for established plants."

Below: Karly in her backyard

As you drive down McBride Drive, an almost grotesque amount of generously sized front lawns surrounds traditional 1960s homes, until you round the corner. There, in the distance, grows an example of hope and change. Karly Silicani's home garden boldly announces itself as an attractive alternative to resource-guzzling lawns, showing that grass could be a feature of the past and that dynamic, colorful, waterwise, and wildlife-friendly gardens are the future.

Karly describes herself as a plant enthusiast with an insatiable curiosity and a stickler for details—true markings of a great garden designer. And even though for Karly this is another career pivot (landscape design being her third), she is unwaveringly passionate about low-water, climate-appropriate plants and using local materials when possible. "On a most basic level, I'm very driven by the idea that gardens should respond to the logic of place, a reference in *The Bold Dry Garden* [a book published in 2016 about Ruth and RBG] that really stuck with me. Ruth's hand was a bit forced, being limited to the water available on-site, but forced or not, responding to the reality of a garden's climate and reasonably available resources is important."

It's not surprising that Karly uses the Ruth Bancroft Garden as inspiration and a reference point in her garden designs, especially on how to use boulders and create meaningful and sweet plant vignettes. Karly explains, "I find myself walking through Ruth's garden in my head when thinking of plant combinations and I imagine a mature version of a plant from her garden before specifying one for a design." RBG is one of only a few places where Karly can see mature plant specimens that she likes to use in a designed setting. Some favorites of hers are the extensive aloes (rare and common), aeoniums, *Brachychiton*, *Chilopsis*, yuccas, *Aristolochia*, and *Garrya*. Karly occasionally even sends clients to RBG for a look around and asks what resonates with them.

When Karly designed her own garden, of course she immediately removed the two thousand-square-foot lawn. Then, similar to what Ruth did, Karly mounded her beds, creating berms that both added some dimension to a very

The ranch style home nestles into the waterwise landscaping. The redwood trees (planted by the original homeowners in the 1970s) also provide shade during the hottest portion of the day.

flat space and mitigated the brutally hard clay. By building up the soil, Karly boosted her confidence in testing finicky plants such as *Protea*, *Banksia*, and *Hakea*, which demand sharp drainage. She also added other favorite sun-loving, low-water plants to this mix with the intention of treating her garden as a laboratory to experiment and trial run new plants.

To achieve her waterwise and money-wise space, Karly only buys four-inch or one-gallon plants, and rarely a five-gallon. By being choosy about sizes, Karly can save money and, just like Ruth and her choice of smaller containers, witness a plant's growth through the various stages of maturity to better understand its quirky habits and cultural needs before using them in client jobs. "I really push my garden to its limits, with no winter protection and the lowest possible irrigation setting."

Karly tests the limits with plants, but she also surreptitiously tests her neighbors. "I suppose in some way my garden is proof to myself, neighbors, and clients that even a family with young kids can have a usable front yard without a lawn." And design wise, this

Melianthus major and *Lomandra* 'Platinum Beauty' create a stellar combination.

A glimpse inside Karly's greenhouse or, as she calls it, her refuge. "Rain or shine, there's always something to do in there. I can check on and water existing plants or, if I'm more ambitious on a certain day, I can tackle propagating, repotting, etc. It houses a plant collection that can't quite swing our cold winter or hot summer temperatures, so I guess it's somewhere between climate denial and nurturing plants until they can handle our climate."

poses a challenge for Karly, seeing as how the neighborhood is more replete with lawns than anything. So occasionally Karly feels a bit timid about using bold textures/forms like those famed backbone plants at RBG. "But a visit to RBG usually helps me snap out of that because there are so many incredible uses of bold textures, especially when those forms juxtapose softer shapes."

In Karly's own garden she also introduced a more diverse habitat that now includes an impressive amount of wildlife. Monarchs munch on milkweed, ladybugs visit mallows, quail families dash and dart between *Lomandra*, lizards bask on boulders, and pipevine swallowtails and skippers frequent her native *Glandularia*. You probably will also catch Karly and her family out front on a bug hunt, playing tag, watching the wildlife, or chatting it up with neighbors. "I like to think that as my garden grows in, it becomes more accessible to our neighbors, and they appreciate what we are doing and the care we put into it."

A soothing sanctuary in the backyard for relaxing and enjoying the sound of the water feature

Mimicking Nature

LANDSCAPE DESIGNER AND CONTRACTOR: Ryan Penn of Specified Horticulture

HOME OF: Marc and Sung-hee Gallo, Walnut Creek, California • USDA ZONE: 9a

After spending nearly a decade working as a horticulturist at the Ruth Bancroft Garden, it's beyond safe to say that Ruth and the garden rubbed off on (actually, more imprinted on) Ryan Penn in regard to both his plant palette and his "Ruthian design principles." Turns out that RBG exposed Ryan to genera that he would later become devoted to, such as cycads, cacti, agaves, and aloes and the near-relative *Gasteria*. But it appears that the influence goes far beyond exposure to specific plant types. "RBG's impact is way more open, exploratory, and experimental, just like how Ruth gardened."

Opposite: Silvery greens playing nicely together. Shown: *Agave montana*, *Hesperaloe parviflora* 'Brakelights', and *Agave nickelsiae*

Below: Ryan in his client's garden

Plants, surprisingly, were at first a latent interest for Ryan, who is now a serious plant enthusiast and garden designer. This avenue germinated and grew into an obsession after undergraduate school, then flowered into a preoccupation during graduate school, eventually bearing fruit when he worked for RBG. The California native flora interest that Ryan also possesses arose from extensive exploration in the California hinterlands. He then took his appreciation of unusual California natives, especially chaparral and desert flora, and Australian and South African shrubs, and enthusiastically added some into RBG's collection. "My goal was to naturalize Ruth's aesthetic with varying low-water tapestries, making use of the drainage potential of the mounds combined with many just recently available xeric plants."

As to how Ryan initially came to RBG, he shares, "I'm from a nearby city and Ruth's garden is the vanguard of the possible in the region, so I was a visitor. I had been working with Troy McGregor for years, including time at Markham Arboretum, and was eventually brought along after Troy started working at RBG."

When Ryan designs gardens for clients, he considers the needs of the individual space while also creating a natural and painterly scene reminiscent of RBG. "I combine a naturalized aesthetic with organizing principles derived from impressionism—loose but structural, without grids or straight lines, always with a sense of movement and an extreme attention to color, texture, and architectural contrast."

Left: A meandering flagstone pathway is softened by silvery *Epilobium septentrionale* 'Wayne's Silver' and punctuated by bold *Agave ovatifolia* (seedling).

Right: The front of the house spotlights a spectacular *Cercidium* ×'Sonoran Emerald' underplanted with *Dasylirion wheeleri*, sharp *Agave parrasana* 'Fireball', and pinky *Aloe capitata*.

For the Gallo Garden, the front yard consisted of a lawn with flax in the middle island and borders, and the back contained a pathway with little else. What ensued was a garden intently inspired by RBG, per the client's request and, of course, Ryan's direct experience. Rocks and boulders were brought in to naturalize the space and intonate movement, coupled with outcroppings of choice plants nodding to the Southwest desert, northern Mexico, and Baja California. "Rocks mimic the mineral soil habitat most of the plants hail from, often growing right on or next to a rock or boulder and acting as the stage from which the plants can perform."

The rear garden creatively transformed into a native plant–infused space where the homeowners relax and socialize while also being entertained by plants offering something interesting yearlong. Ryan's "Bancroft-esque" plant painting sinuously moves across the space and breaks up the challenging long fence and preexisting flagstone path. The other challenge for Ryan was the diminutive planting borders, as they made it difficult to naturalize due to a lack of depth.

The design solution? Ryan emphasized the placement of architectural elements with a minimalist palette, focusing on specimens to augment interest, such as a *Dioon*, manzanitas, and *Mestoklema*, with *Epilobium septentrionale* 'Select Mattole' providing needed continuity. Other key design elements are the three important *Agave ovatifolia*, barely fitting into their allotted space but providing anchors for "turns" in the linear path.

Ryan praises Ruth for being an incredibly adventurous and open gardener, always on the lookout for the novel and unusual, and ready to experiment, with plenty of failure to be expected. "In my own gardening and growing, if not plant choices for clients, this open and experimental stance is paramount. In any garden I design, I try to bring this natural yet painterly scene to life, melded with the individuated space of the particular place."

A cluster of California native buckwheats and California fuchsia soften the path and the sharpness of the nearby agaves. Shown: *Agave ovatifolia* (seedling), *Agave* 'Blue Glow', *Epilobium septentrionale* 'Wayne's Silver', *Eriogonum latifolium* × *E. rubescens*, and *E. grande* var. *rubescens*.

Year-Round Rhythm and Texture

LANDSCAPE DESIGNER: Kristin Caldwell Garden Design

LANDSCAPE CONTRACTOR: Kristin and Mark Caldwell

HOME OF: Kristin and Mark Caldwell, Moraga, California • **USDA ZONE:** 9b

Sometimes new careers present themselves, and a handful of people turn a cheek and reject the offer while others willingly (also a wee bit cautiously) take them on and make the shift. In 1991, such was the case for Kristin Caldwell, who acquired a garden maintenance business from a friend who was moving away. This might sound like a fantastically fortuitous opportunity, but Kristin possessed little to no experience in this field. After instantly realizing how much she needed to learn about plants, she enrolled in design and horticulture classes at Merritt College. This much-needed education ignited Kristin's interest so much that she dove further into the horticultural world by extending her services to include design work for her maintenance clients. Eventually, with a few design jobs in line, Kristin assembled her plant aesthetic and gravitated toward sustainable plants that didn't depend on regular water to look good and survive.

Kristin's go-to plant list blossomed after she visited RBG, where she immediately fell in love with the boldness and symmetry of the agaves, especially *Agave franzosinii*. Kristin shares, "Of course these big agaves can only live in a big space, so to create the same effect but on a smaller scale I started using more manageable agaves, such as *Agave* 'Blue Glow', *A.* 'Blue Flame', *A. lophantha* 'Quadricolor', *A.* ×'Little Shark', and *A. parryi* 'Cream Spike'." Over the years, and after repeated visits to RBG, Kristin broadened her plant favorites even more and now embraces more Australian (*Eucalyptus*, *Hakea*, and *Banksia*) and South African plants (*Leucadendron* and *Leucospermum*).

Opposite: An embrace of different hues of blue foliage, coupled with the profuse lavender-pink *Oscularia deltoides* blooms and the magenta-pink *Calandrinia spectabilis*, pairs well with the *Leucospermum* 'Scarlet Ribbon' and deep red *Hesperaloe* bloom.

For her clients' gardens, Kristin's plant palette has now largely evolved to incorporate low-water or very low–water plants, as she has discovered that even moderately thirsty plants struggle more than they did five years ago. And she leans on RBG for continued inspiration regarding the use of bold plantings that both repeat for a satisfactory rhythm and that balance out softer textures. "I feel that Ruth didn't plant solely for bloom (though she certainly appreciated them in her irises) but rather for vegetative form, color, and texture. I do that as well in my planting designs as that gives the garden more structure and year-round appeal."

Kristin enjoys playing with complementary colors such as green, yellow, and purple. "I like a structured hardscape design but also adding softness with plants that trail over and into the rigid lines." Kristin also likes adding elements such as these hypertufa pots and steel birdbath to soften some of the sharp corners.

The back garden not only displays a diversity in color and texture, but multiple outdoor rooms are created and separated by thoughtful hardscape and soft plantings.

Adding to this, Kristin is not timid in her choices. "I'm not afraid to use plants that aren't well known to the public but have proven to be tough and beautiful in the landscape trade." This forward-thinking approach to designing also wove its way into Kristin's personal garden. When it came time to design her own space, Kristin wholeheartedly embraced dry plants, experimenting with various species to see what would survive the blazing heat and cold dips into the midtwenties. She also likes those that thrive on a bit of unintentional neglect. To achieve this balance, Kristin incorporated hardy plants like echeverias, aloes, hakeas, acacias, and yuccas.

Design wise, Kristin's backyard is wide but shallow, so to make the area feel more spacious she created separate and distinct rooms, employed bluestone pavers, raised concrete

Above left: Kristin relaxes with Yalla the granddog, who is the most loyal and excited garden visitor and proficient at rodent patrol.

Above right: A lovely repetition of pinks, greens, and grays is provided by *Echeveria* 'Afterglow', *Westringia fruticosa* 'Grey Box', and *Spiraea japonica* 'Limemound'.

edging, and raised planters, and built an ipe deck, wood arbor, and a privacy wall constructed of twin wall (normally used in commercial greenhouses).

In the mornings, like a sun-seeking cat, Kristin gravitates toward the front flagstone patio to enjoy her coffee, soaking in some rays while observing bird antics in the verdant palo verde. Then, in the evenings after work, Kristin migrates to the backyard when the setting sun backlights the batu fence, making the garden glow. But in honesty, she explains, "I don't really linger much in my garden as there is always something to take care of. A garden really is never done. It takes time for it to grow into the vision you have, and then something, either by choice or nature, can change a part of it. I usually look at it as an opportunity to try something new and learn from it."

Kristin shares, "The white *Yucca filamentosa* 'Color Guard' blooms are spectacular for a few weeks but it's the *Leucadendron* 'Safari Sunset' with its deep red bracts forming in late summer and lasting through winter that gives the garden a much-needed punch of color."

Mounding for Interest

SELF-DESIGNED HOME GARDEN OF: Kipp McMichael and his husbands, Berkeley, California • USDA ZONE: 10b

Ashby Avenue (State Highway 13) is a major artery in the flatlands of Berkeley, which means this road is busy, fast-paced, and generally bordered by parked cars. This explains why not many people notice Kipp McMichael's garden as they speed down this two-lane thoroughfare. But they should. (Side note: we really try to train ourselves not to gaze at gardens while driving.)

By trade, Kipp is a web developer, but he calls himself a "hortiphile" by passion. And it is magically serendipitous how plant people find each other sometimes. Kipp moved to California and by chance rented a home from a man who had a similar passion for succulents and arid plants. To further the meant-to-be, on move-in day Kipp met his landlord's friend, none other than Brian Kemble. Soon after, Kipp ventured to RBG. "Those early visits to RBG taught me the value of large statement plants juxtaposed with smaller companions. I could see examples of the kinds of succulents that thrive in the Bay Area."

Being resourceful and enthused, Kipp amassed a large collection of succulent planters on the roof deck of his San Francisco apartment. "That was great practice for gardening in small spaces, and some of those plants, like the now tree-sized *Euphorbia ammak*, got their start in those planters." It was not until ten years later in 2010 that Kipp finally got a full garden space of his own to indulge and deep dive into his passion for succulents.

When Kipp moved into his new home, the level yard consisted of flowering shrubs and perennials, so he immediately denuded everything via a "free if you dig them up yourself" post on Craigslist. Once a blank canvas existed, Kipp hauled in ten tons of rock and soil (a gravelly blend of equal parts pumice, coarse sand, granite, and potting mix) and created a large mound he affectionately calls "Mt. Ashby" on a diagonal arc through the main bed. In the smaller bed that sits against the front of the house, Kipp built a retaining wall to create a mounded bed and to protect the siding and foundation. Blessed with a frost-free front yard and succulent-pleasing eastern and southern exposures, Kipp planted a variety of xeric beauties.

No garden is ever finished, stationary, or immune to upheavals, and such is the case with Kipp's garden. After years of lax weeding, a *Dasylirion longissimum* and some agaves and yuccas becoming too rambunctious for such a little space, and the dreaded pandemic

Opposite: What the front garden lacks in size, it makes up for in plant density. Shown: *Cordyline australis*, *Aloe ferox*, *Beaucarnea recurvata*, *Echeveria agavoides* 'Scarlet', *Agave victoria-reginae*, *Euphorbia anoplia*, *Deuterocohnia brevifolia*, *Echeveria agavoides* 'Lipstick', and *Agave* 'Kissho Kan'

Above left: *Kippus plantnerdicus* stands proudly under a mature *Cordyline australis*.

Above right: The exuberant home colorfully complements the plant-filled front. Shown: *Agonis flexuosa*, *Brachychiton rupestris*, *Agave* 'Blue Glow', *Aloe ferox*, *Cordyline australis*, *Aloidendron barberae*, *Encephalartos trispinosus*, and *Corymbia citriodora*

crashing down on the world, Kipp started his "Covid Project" in 2022. This involved a major overhaul of the entire garden, including adding two feet to Mt. Ashby and annexing the neglected sidewalk strip next door.

Looking to feed his hunger to get planting and refresh his garden, Kipp dove into the expanded and diverse plant offerings of the nursery at RBG. (Several of Kipp's own seed-grown South African *Amaryllis* are now part of RBG collection.) Kipp also admits to scouring the racks at Home Depot in San Rafael. He claims you can find real treasures for a small price.

"My garden is a product of limited space and wanting one of everything," Kipp says. All his beds embrace some form of mounding for visual interest, mimicking how hills and mountains lend drama to a large landscape. But most importantly for Kipp, "It allows me to plant more plants in less space, and many plants such as succulents look particularly nice staged in the nooks and crannies of a rocky slope."

It's no surprise that Kipp faces the inevitable problem of theft due to the garden being front and center on a bustling street. He shares, "The constant traffic has one silver lining in that it helps discourage theft since people think there are always so many eyes on my garden."

Every nook and cranny in Kipp's front mounded garden are intentionally occupied. Shown: *Mangave* 'Silver Fox', *Euphorbia esculenta inermis*, *Agave victoria-reginae* subsp. *swobodae*, *Gasteria* 'White Ice', *Aloe* 'Christmas Sleigh', *Euphorbia anoplia*, *Deuterocohnia lorentziana*, and *Echeveria* 'Perle von Nurnberg'. Kipp shares, "The *Senecio rowleyanus* takes regular trimming to prevent it swamping the low/slow-growing plants around it."

The raised bed (aka Mt. Ashby) populated with larger and noticeably vertical plants helps screen out the busy street. Shown: *Aloe* hybrid, *Phormium* sp., *Chorisia speciosa*, *Aloe ramosissima*, *Euphorbia leucodendron*, *Encephalartos trispinosus*, and various *Euphorbia* spp.

Connecting to Nature and Beauty

SELF-DESIGNED HOME GARDEN OF: Molly Stone and Michael Cohn, Berkeley, California • USDA ZONE: 9b/10a

Located in the Thousand Oaks neighborhood of North Berkeley sits the house of glass artist Molly Stone and her husband, Michael Cohn. From the street, the lot appears politely small until you walk through the gate and begin heading down the stone stairs. Immediately outcroppings of colossal volcanic Northbrae rhyolite boulders (prevalent in the neighborhood) announce their massive presence and anchor a thoughtful and well-crafted plant paradise.

When Molly and her artist husband bought the house in 1988, ivy and blackberries consumed most of the rocks and garden space, as the property had not been gardened since the construction of the house in 1925. The couple's weekends inevitably consisted of macheting their way through the bramble until they slowly uncovered their massive treasures and then began planning out the dream garden.

The first phase consisted of planting California and Mediterranean native plants such as *Ribes*, *Arbutus*, *Garrya elliptica*, *Rhamnus*, *Sambucus*, and many understory plants to complement the existing sentinel *Quercus agrifolia*. The second phase of the design accelerated after Molly visited UC Santa Cruz Arboretum & Botanic Garden and observed the Australian and South African plant possibilities.

Molly began devouring garden literature and journals, which, of course, then catapulted her to various gardens for inspiration—RBG being one of her visited spots. "I was stunned by Ruth's captivating garden and her story of commitment to her dry garden theme. She opened my eyes to a new kind of Bay Area garden. Plants that I had only seen in desert landscapes were thriving and she had some of my new favorite Australian and South African gems."

Opposite: Even Molly's street-side garden boasts a tapestry of textures for those walking by. Deer luckily leave these low-water lovelies alone. A mass of echeverias dotted with aloes and agaves and grounded by a midsize *Manzanita* provides a vibrant welcome to Molly's visitors.

The third phase of Molly's garden began when many of the Australian plants she had added outgrew their space. She removed numerous overzealous plants, which opened areas to redesign for focal points while also forcing her to tackle the heavy Berkeley clay soil. To remedy the soil situation, Molly installed drainage and added porous soil mixes with grit and less organic matter, making mounds and more mounds. Needing additional

California native *Quercus agrifolia* grows proudly next to one of the tallest personally owned boulders in Berkeley. Shown: *Cercocarpus betuloides*, *Acacia cognata* 'Cousin Itt', *Agave* 'Celsii Nova', *Aloe striata* 'Ghost', *Euphorbia lambii*, *Macrozamia johnsonii*, and various echeverias

Above left: Solid stone stairs wind up through the property and are softened by *Carex testacea* 'Prairie Fire', *Anigozanthos* 'Orange Cross', *Sedum adolphi*, *Dioon edule*, and a substantial *Acacia cultriformis*.

Above right: Molly admits she only feels completely dressed when she dons her garden clippers and holster.

inspiration, Molly went to RBG to see mature plants that were in the running (like agaves and aloes) placed in thoughtful relationships with each other. Molly adds, "I also visited and consulted with the extremely knowledgeable RBG staff, including Brian and Walker."

Like Ruth, Molly would jump in her truck and head south to collect plants, even venturing on plant escapades to dry parts of California to hike and explore and observe plants, stopping along the way to visit nurseries and arboretums and botanical gardens. Molly eventually added to her garden aloes, agaves, cycads, yuccas, echeverias, and euphorbias. She also replaced overhead irrigation with drip or no irrigation and utilized the massive rocks for their ability to create many microclimates where she could tweak and add, artistically expressing herself through blades and petals and color.

"I garden because there is no other thing that I want to do more," Molly says. "It's my favorite focus. Time disappears when I'm in the garden and I am constantly surprised, intrigued, and challenged and in awe and wonder. In the garden I feel connected to life."

A petite path is hugged by an assortment of well-chosen plants, providing year-round color and texture. Included here are *Aeonium* 'Sunburst', *Echeveria* 'Afterglow', *Agave* 'Blue Glow', and *Chamaerops humilis* var. *cerifera*.

Close to the house, a group of huge boulders existed that were inaccessible and dangerous, so during Covid Molly and her husband built a small flagstone patio tucked in between. Now this nook is not only a favorite private space that peeks into the dry garden below and provides a vista of the Golden Gate Bridge, but it's also framed and shaded by one of Molly's favorite plants, *Garrya elliptica*. A simple solution to a problem area added a whole new room to the garden.

Hillside Haven

LANDSCAPE DESIGNER AND CONTRACTOR: Beth Mullins of Growsgreen

HOME OF: Beth Mullins, Oakland, California • USDA ZONE: 9b

On any given day, a multitude of visitors tour and enjoy Beth Mullins's garden in the Oakland hills. And by visitors we mean deer, raccoons, birds, and a bevy of insects. And why wouldn't this garden be a hub? On a significantly sloping site, it is dotted with sixteen small and large coast live oaks that not only help stabilize the soil and contribute rich organic leaf litter, but also create and invite a diverse habitat. Being mindful of these oak canopies and their delicate root systems, Beth created a garden in a challenging space and for the hardest client: herself.

Opposite: *Grevillea* 'Moonlight' attracts pollinators, is long blooming, and very carefree.

Below: Beth in her enclosed vegetable garden

Beth had to keep all the possibilities on the table while also being aware of a self-imposed constricted budget. She needed to start taming the hill and creating functional flat spaces. With the significant grade staring at her, Beth required herself to study the topography for months. She walked the land even before putting pen to paper, so she could determine the best ways to create usable spaces, access paths, and steps, and maximize the views. "Normally I would put the dining area close to the house, but the view is spectacular on the hill and it's a good way to activate the space and get people up there to appreciate it." Her goal: create a garden of calm and subtle interest by ways of levels, transitions, and texture.

Having both a landscape architecture degree and a PhD in biochemistry, Beth is known for designing modern or traditional modern gardens in hilly residential spaces struggling with challenging grades. She tackles steep spaces and solves retaining issues while also creating functional extensions of homes. "I aim for calming the space and it's very important for me to 'solve' a garden hardscape puzzle in a way that works with the existing constraints of the house, fence lines, or grades, and be able to pull out what the grades are already telling me."

Agave americana, *Myoporum parvifolium*, *Olea europaea* 'Bonita', *Sesleria autumnalis*, and *Muhlenbergia lindheimeri* bring interest to a tricky hillside. "I am inspired by RBG to use fluffier plants like *Eriogonum* and euphorbias interspersed with more sculptural plants like agaves. I love how they allow a massing of plants to intersect on the ground plane as well as in the vertical view."

In gardens, Beth appreciates openness but also a sense of entry and intrigue. In her own garden, the space was so long, she created an end point for the lower area to keep the feeling of scale with the surroundings and the visitor. "I like that the rustic wood screen is not a solid block of material and lets in light." This was Beth's first screen that she experimented with before proposing them to clients. Now she frequently uses them in her designs. Shown: Spineless *Opuntia* and *Acacia iteaphylla* softening the edges

Simple stairs lead down through California live oaks, *Pennisetum spathiolatum*, and *Sesleria autumnalis*. Daniel Velasquez, a local muralist and potter, designed and painted the floral mural art.

Beth also incorporates waterwise plants to support the architectural elements she designs, finding that sculptural dry plants perfectly complement a clean-lined hardscape. So naturally RBG is a teaching tool for Beth, showing her how certain species can alter a perception of what a traditional garden should be and what the ingredients are. Beth comments that Ruth was way ahead of her time, and her approach to using waterwise plants has informed the Bay Area and beyond. Beth also shares what she finds most inspiring about the Ruth Bancroft Garden: "RBG highlights interesting plants that can take the place of many desired ornamental herbaceous plants and provide everyone with a sustainable alternative that is not only beautiful but will thrive in the drought climate of California."

Even though Beth had to enclose her vegetable garden because of nibbling deer and ravaging racoons, she designed an attractive and modern solution. Shown: *Sabal* sp., *Agave* sp., and *Heteromeles arbutifolia* (volunteer). Beth shares, "I kept all the volunteers and live oaks existing in the garden."

Eriogonum and *Asclepia*, for example, were two plants Beth didn't fully appreciate until she saw them in situ at RBG, and she now believes they should be in every garden. And for her own garden, Beth incorporates tried-and-true plants as a backdrop, so a sense of cohesion exists. She also adds experimental drought-tolerant plants, specifically ones she doesn't grow in clients' gardens. "I wanted to leave room to study things as they grow…or fail, all while keeping the garden looking its best"—a very Ruthian approach.

For Beth it's clear that it's not just about liking the shape and structure of low-water plants. "With the climate changing to drier and drier in the West," she says, "in order to have an ornamental garden we have to be stewards of the land and water. Growing low-water plants is essential and responsible and, in my opinion, the only option."

A Glimpse of Home

LANDSCAPE DESIGNER AND CONTRACTOR: Troy McGregor of Gondwana Flora

HOME OF: Troy and Vicki McGregor, Martinez, California • USDA ZONE: 9b

Turns out that to be an adult plant enthusiast or landscape designer, you didn't have to be a superfan of plants as a child. Such is the case with Troy McGregor, who, despite growing up on two acres in North Queensland, Australia, among a myriad of tropical fruit trees, palms, and flowering trees, didn't view this plant-filled experience as paradise. Quite the opposite is true, Troy explains: "Our property was a blank slate when we moved there, and my job was mowing and carrying heavy buckets of water to trees that didn't have irrigation." Grueling garden work can, of course, potentially damper positive feelings. "In a nutshell, I didn't care much for plants. And now, as I think about it, this explains why I hate doing garden maintenance."

Ironically, and all thanks to Troy, the Ruth Bancroft Garden now contains an impressive assortment of Australian and Proteaceae plants. In the past, Ruth tried growing Australian natives, but many weren't suitable due to the soil conditions and colder conditions. Troy shares, "I started looking for, and growing, varieties that would do well in RBG. Fortunately, and watch me jinx this, the cold spells that caused so much havoc in the garden in years past didn't seem to be as much of an issue." Troy added (via the garden staff) different varieties of *Banksia*, *Leucospermum*, and *Hakea*, as well as some oddballs like *Cantua volcanica* and *Freylinia undulata*. The prize, according to Troy, is *Hakea lehmanniana*, with its steel-blue flowers.

Troy also, at one point, became RBG's full-time nursery manager, and his contributions during that time are still alive today, specifically his suggestion for creating a year-round retail nursery. Troy saw that RBG didn't have a full-fledged nursery, and the fact that their big one-day sales were so successful proved that an appetite for the plants RBG showcased existed. "Luckily the board was willing to try out my ideas and so the transformation of the nursery began. I started buying plants to supplement the ones our volunteers were propagating, as well as imported seed from South Africa and Australia."

During this time, Troy also did simple design work for RBG to help plant sales. Naturally these clients would then ask Troy for referrals to install his plans, and because most of the installation work was too small or the plants too new (or too scary) for some landscape companies, Troy saw an opportunity to fill a void. Troy pitched an idea to the board of

Opposite: To create privacy and street-side interest, Troy artfully layered evergreen plants. Shown: *Hakea archaeoides*, *H. petiolaris*, *Aloe striata* hybrid, *Lomandra confertifolia* ssp. *rubiginosa* 'Seascape', *Banksia blechnifolia*, *Aloe* 'Moonglow', and *Leucadendron* 'Ebony'.

Tucked behind a low concrete wall, an inviting but semiprivate seating area is where Troy and his wife eat on the weekends during the summer months.

directors of RBG about starting a landscape installation service to complement what RBG was already doing, but at that point RBG couldn't commit. Troy was now at a junction: remain as nursery manager or explore the opportunity to do installations. "I chose the latter and Gondwana Flora was born."

Remember how young Troy wasn't a plant fan? Well, his first "aha" moment came later when he helped with propagation at a nonprofit nursery and witnessed a seed germinate and turn into a plant. "I was just amazed with the magic of taking a stick, dipping it in some dust (rooting powder), poking it in some soil, and within a few months it had roots. I was hooked!" Troy, realizing that he possessed proficiency at this "plant growing nonsense" and that this activity was far more enjoyable than sitting in an office, finally decided to start growing plants.

This plant-growing nonsense became super handy when he later started his landscape company, because otherwise he couldn't source many of the plants he liked to use in his garden designs (Australian, South African, and other southern hemisphere plants). As it

A narrow space and a ho-hum wall can be transformed when upright pots and a vine enter the scene. Vine: *Passiflora* 'Blue Horizon'. Gray pots: *Euphorbia lambii* and *Mangrave* 'Bad Hair Day'. Green pot: *Agave* 'Snow Glow'.

Above left: Troy with his canine friend Clary

Above right: Troy created a mounded bed á la Ruth complete with undemanding favorites. Shown: *Acca sellowiana*, *Crassula sarcocaulis*, *Encephalartos lehmannii*, *Aloe capitata* var. *quartziticola*, *Aeonium nobile*, and *Aloe glauca* 'Namaqualand'.

turns out, Troy is a bit addicted now. "I can't imagine not planting a seed or taking a cutting. Too much in my DNA."

When you visit Troy's home garden, you get a glimpse of his home country through the garden created in a very grassroots kind of way. With zero horticultural training or experience at the time, Troy decided to, in his words, "blank slate it except for the trees." The demo included removing an excess of red bricks and a thirsty, tired lawn. For the front garden, Troy designed a forty-foot curving concrete wall to divide the space and create a separation from the street and an intimate seating area. At first, he planted many California natives but eventually removed a bulk of them and added his favorite Australian and South African plants.

For his backyard, Troy knew he wanted the space to be more intimate for him and his wife, and it should be used primarily for eating and growing vegetables. With that wish list, and to introduce interest, he created a multilevel bermed and bouldered space á la Bancroft. Naturally, Troy gained inspiration from being immersed in the tapestry of succulents at RBG, so he added many varieties to his home collection. "I had so many nooks and crannies that other plants just wouldn't do well in. Succulents played well with my Gondwana plants and created a lush look." Many changes ensued in his back garden over the years, including the addition in 2020 of the "Pandemic Chooks" (aka a chicken coop).

Troy is one of the listed designers for the local water district and helps homeowners switch over from thirsty grass to a glorious and regionally appropriate garden. Through his design process, Troy shares that he always tries to remain "horticulturally curious," a phrase Dick Turner, the first executive director of RBG when it became public, coined to describe Ruth. And to help guide him deeper into the depths of dry plants, Troy reflects on the lessons learned through RBG. "I'm continually inspired by the multidimensionality, layers of ground covers all the way up to the tree canopies, and the borrowed scenery from other beds viewed through gaps in the foreground. Those are magic and I always try to think about this when transforming gardens."

Nearly two decades, and thousands of notable plants later, Troy still finds amazement with how a tiny seed can magically transform into a plant. Truly an appreciation for the small things in life that sometimes end up being the big things.

Even a typical narrow driveway is enlivened with colorful plants such as *Cordyline fruticosa* 'Glauca', *Prostanthera ovalifolia* 'Variegata', and *Leucospermum grandiflorum*.

The Wilds of Walnut Creek

LANDSCAPE DESIGNER: Cricket Riley of Lush Dry Gardens

LANDSCAPE CONTRACTOR: Rodolfo Castro

NATURAL SWIMMING POOL EQUIPMENT: BioNova Natural Pools

NATURAL POOL EQUIPMENT INSTALLATION: Bay Area Koi Ponds

HOME OF: Cricket, Robert, Josephine, and Genevieve Riley, Walnut Creek, California • USDA ZONE: 9a

Imagine being born in a house on stilts, perched over fog-filled Tomales Bay. This scenario begins to describe Cricket Riley's hippy/beatnik childhood. Cricket's mother was a painter and her father the drummer of the 1960's folk rock band The Youngbloods, whose 1967 hit "Get Together" was an anthem for the Summer of Love. Cricket shares, "I was given the impression from a young age that it was important to try to make the world better." As a landscape designer and lecturer, Cricket strives to realize this in her clients' gardens as well as her own. Through her thoughtful, climate-appropriate and waterwise plant and hardscape choices, she is making her parents' given responsibility a reality.

Opposite: Cricket Riley's highly textured garden

Below: Cricket in her garden

Cricket's deep appreciation for nature, plants, and gardens goes way back. "My love for plants started in childhood, although I didn't realize it until after I started in this field." Growing up in the wilds of West Marin without a TV and spending hours playing in the woods and creek by her house, Cricket grew up feeling at home digging in the dirt. "My mother loved gardening, but I actually hated it as a teenager because she made me weed as part of my weekly chores. My teenage self would be very surprised to see me now."

Out of high school Cricket studied history at University of California, Santa Cruz. She then got her master's at New York University in broadcast journalism and Near Eastern studies before spending some time working on the news desk at CNN in Los Angeles. After moving around for a bit, she eventually settled with her own family in Walnut Creek. They purchased an untouched Eichler overrun with twelve thousand square feet of unruly ivy, juniper, and vinca.

Top: Where once was a front lawn now grows a dense planting of shrubs and agaves with a restrained color palette that also provides visitors with a quiet yet energetic display.

Bottom: The curving paths and beds provide a nice balance to the mid-century architecture of the Eichler home.

The floor-to-ceiling windows bring the garden into the home.

The swimming pool is natural—meaning no chlorine or salt are used to disinfect the water. Instead, it is cleaned mechanically with two filter systems, gravel, and UV light. It's like swimming in a clean pond. Did you know that pool chemicals are bad for the environment? Their production and distribution, as well as the overflow and off-gassing once in the water, are all environmental pollutants. Natural pools, on the other hand, are sustainable and don't need monthly maintenance. When you need to flush the water out of the retention area (where the gravel and filters live), it can be used to water plants. The tiles are seconds from the Heath Tile Shed in Sausalito.

Serendipitously, the Ruth Bancroft Garden is only a couple of blocks from Cricket's house, and it is at RBG where she discovered her plant template. But there was a small problem: Cricket possessed minimal gardening skills. She began experimenting in her garden with plants from the sale section of RBG nursery. She says, "One of the first things that struck me from the beginning about the Ruth Bancroft Garden was the idea of planting for the microclimate you are gardening in. Ruth planted what would thrive with the least amount of water and maintenance. Planting for where you are and the climate you are in is how we should all be gardening. Being sustainable in your garden is the ultimate in "Think global, act local."

Through her home garden renovation process, and after many hours volunteering in the garden at her kids' schools, Cricket realized that she wanted to design gardens as a career. She enrolled in the landscape architecture A.A. program at Merritt College and shortly after began working at RBG. Once Cricket graduated, she launched the landscape design department at RBG.

Walnut Creek is no stranger to large lawns and thirsty landscapes, but serious potential and change exist. As more people open up to the idea of replacing their lawns with gardens, Cricket and her team are uniquely positioned to help with that process. "Take one of those lawns and turn it into a beautiful, rambling, blooming, habitat-supporting garden and the next thing you know everyone is going to want one."

Cricket designed her home garden with three different factors in mind. The first is her woodsy, free-spirited upbringing, which plays out in the garden's relaxed, naturalistic, and homey feel. "I really like wild, natural places, so my garden is an effort to create that in the suburbs." As a gardener who prefers a denser planting, Cricket squeezes in many of her favorite plants (a good number are California natives) to mimic the wildness of the creeks and valleys of West Marin. However, since Walnut Creek is hotter, drier, and colder due to being farther inland, the plant choices are at times slightly different. "I love California native *Atriplex lentiformis* with its crazy silvery brambleness that is kind of a beast and grows large and dense with little water." The same favoritism is true for *Sphaeralcea*, *Salvia*, and *Muhlenbergia rigens* because these low-water California natives can produce a "lush" feel if planted densely and occasionally cut back.

The second influence for her garden was the architecture of the house. Designed by A. Quincy Jones and Frederick Emmons as one of thousands built by Joseph Eichler in the post–World War II housing boom, the mid-century modern house is boxy in shape with walls of floor-to-ceiling windows that face the back garden. "I wanted the garden to be a foil for the house, a wild, naturalistic planting that is a contrast to the very simple architecture." The windows also played a key role in how the beds were laid out and the plants arranged in them. "Views into the garden are important in these homes because of the walls of glass. You feel like you are in the garden when you are sitting on the couch in your living room or eating at your dining room table. It's fun to look out the windows and see the jungle."

The last influence on Cricket's home garden is, of course, RBG, which announces itself in the graphic and architectural shapes and the low-water and climate-appropriate plant choices. "Combining agaves, palms, cacti, and yuccas with soft, leafy California, Australian, and South African native plants is completely taken from RBG. Ruth's understanding of the natural form of plants inspires me to this day." Cricket also knows that if certain plants do well in RBG, then they will do as equally as well in her garden, given the same growing conditions. The goal and purpose of Cricket's garden are layered. "I wanted to create a place of respite while also experimenting with plants. I like to try plants out before I put them in the clients' gardens. Personal experience is the best indicator of success."

"I've always loved palm trees," Cricket says, "and in the last few years I've accumulated a nice collection of low-water/frost-tolerant ones." She adores how graphic and architectural the leaves are, the sounds they make in the wind, and the classical reference of the palm in the garden throughout Europe and the Middle East. "I think palms bring an elegance to a garden and they work in just about any garden style."

Recommended Resources

A word on plant nomenclature: All plant names are listed to the best of our ability and accuracy at the time of writing this book. It's important to understand that botanical names constantly change.

The databases that we refer to:

San Marcos Growers Nursery Plant Database: SMGrowers.com

Calscape: Calscape.org/search

And, lastly, Brian Kemble (RBG Curator), who is well versed in the nomenclature of this plant palette and has a huge resource of reference books.

Books

Can a gardener have too many garden books? We don't think so. Here are some of our favorites:

Baldwin, Debra Lee. *Designing with Succulents*. Portland, OR: Timber Press, 2007.

Baldwin, Debra Lee. *Succulent Container Gardens: Design Eye-Catching Displays With 350 Easy-Care Plants*. Portland, OR: Timber Press, 2010.

Booth, Norman, and James Hiss. *Residential Landscape Architecture: Design Process for the Private Residence*. London: Pearson, 2011.

Brenzel, Kathleen Norris. *Sunset Western Garden Book of Easy-Care Plantings*. New York: Time Inc. Books, 2015.

Church, Thomas, Grace Hall, and Michael Laurie. *Gardens Are for People*. Oakland: University of California Press, 1995.

Dewees, Jason. *Designing with Palms*. Portland, OR: Timber Press, 2018.

Dortort, Fred. *The Timber Press Guide to Succulent Plants of the World: A Comprehensive Reference to More Than 2000 Species*. Portland, OR: Timber Press, 2011.

Opposite: A September evening in Karly Silicani's garden

Eaton, Isa, and Jennifer Kramer. *Small Garden Style: A Design Guide for Outdoor Rooms and Containers*. Emeryville, CA: Ten Speed Press, 2020.

Gentry, Howard. *Agaves of Continental North America*. Tucson: University of Arizona Press, 1982.

Harlow, Nora. *Gardening in Summer Dry Climates: Plants for a Lush, Water-Conscious Landscape*. Portland, OR: Timber Press, 2021.

Hatch, Charles. *Trees of the California Landscape: A Photographic Manual of Native and Ornamental Trees*. Oakland: University of California Press, 2007.

Irish, Gary and Mary. *Agaves, Yuccas, and Related Plants: A Gardener's Guide*. Portland, OR: Timber Press, 2000.

Lowenfels, Jeff, and Wayne Lewis. *Teaming With Microbes: The Organic Gardener's Guide to the Soil Food Web*. Portland, OR: Timber Press, 2010.

Matthews, Lewis. *Protea: A Guide to Cultivated Species and Varieties*. Honolulu: Latitude 20, 2016.

McLennan, Rob. *Growing Proteas*. Nashville: Kangaroo Press, 1994.

Moore, Jeff. *Aloes & Agaves in Cultivation*. N.p.: self-published, 2016.

Moore, Jeff. *Soft Succulents: Aeoniums, Echeverias, Crassulas, Sedums, Kalanchoes, and Related Plants*. N.p.: self-published, 2016.

Moore, Jeff. *Spiny Succulents: Euphorbias, Cacti, and Other Sculptural Succulents and (Mostly) Spiny Xerophytic Plants*. N.p.: self-published, 2016.

Newton, L. E., S. Carter, J. J. Lavranos, and C. C. Walker. *Aloes: The Definitive Guide*. Richmond, UK: Royal Botanic Gardens, Kew, 2021.

Nolan, Daniel. *Dry Gardens: High Style for Low Water Gardens*. New York: Rizzoli, 2018.

Perry, Robert. *Landscape Plants for California Gardens*. N.p.: Land Design Pub., 2010.

Preston-Mafham, Rod. *Cacti: The Illustrated Dictionary*. Portland, OR: Timber Press, 1997.

Ritter, Matt. *A Californian's Guide to the Trees Among Us*. Berkeley: Heyday, 2016.

Rubin, Greg, and Lucy Warren. *The Drought-Defying California Garden: 230 Native Plants for a Lush, Low-Water Landscape*. Portland, OR: Timber Press, 2016.

Silver, Johanna. *The Bold Dry Garden*. Portland, OR: Timber Press, 2016. (This is a fantastic reference on Ruth and the RBG garden that we adore.)

Slatalla, Michelle. *Gardenista: The Definitive Guide to Stylish Outdoor Spaces*. New York: Artisan, 2016.

Star, Greg. *Agaves: Living Sculptures for Landscapes and Containers*. Portland, OR: Timber Press, 2012.

Stewart, Angus, and AB Bishop. *The Waterwise Australian Native Garden*. Sydney: Murdoch Books, 2019.

Stockwell, Robin. *Succulents: The Ultimate Guide to Choosing, Designing, and Growing 200 Easy Care Plants*. Chicago: TI Inc. Books, 2017.

Thompkins, Peter, and Christopher Bird. *The Secret Life of Plants*. New York: Harper & Row, 1989.

Van Wyck, Ben-Erik, and Gideon Smith. *Guide to the Aloes of South Africa*. Pretoria: Briza Publications, 2012.

Yetman, David. *The Great Cacti: Ethnobotany & Biogeography*. Tucson: University of Arizona Press, 2008.

Online Resources

Just like books, you can never have enough helpful resources to lean on and learn from. The same goes for visiting nurseries where we all could wander for hours. The list below is for the perennial student who can't seem to get enough. Consider us like a doting mom feeding your plant passion.

CalScape (Calscape.org)
Contra Costa Water District (CCWater.com)
East Bay Municipal Utility District (EBMUD.com)
Greywater Action (GreywaterAction.org)
Monrovia Nursery (Monrovia.com)
Plant Lust (PlantLust.com)
Ruth Bancroft Garden & Nursery (RuthBancroftGarden.org)
San Marcos Growers (SMGrowers.com)
Summer Dry Project (Summer-Dry.com)
Theodore Payne Foundation (TheodorePayne.org)
Water Use Classification of Landscape Species (CCUH.UCDavis.edu/wucols)
Waterwise Garden Planner (WaterWiseGardenPlanner.org)

Acknowledgments

We would like to thank our families, who perennially give us strength, encouragement, inspiration, and always comedic relief. This book would not be possible without the beautiful images by Caitlin Atkinson. We are forever indebted to you.

We would also like to thank this group of supportive, knowledgeable, creative, and inspiring people: Brian Kemble, Walker Young, Nikki Vroom, Kate Nowell, Becky Perrine, Sarah Nelson, and Monica Avila.

Thanks also to:
All the other Ruth Bancroft Garden staff
From Timber Press: Sarah Milhollin, Makenna Goodman, Jacoba Lawson, Pam Kingsley, and Stacee Lawrence
The Merritt College Landscape Horticulture Program
All the featured homeowners and designers

Opposite: Max Cannon's colorful front garden

Index

Opposite: Lacy pink leaves of *Echeveria* play off the blooming *Dorycnium hirsutum*.

N

O

P

Q

R

From left to right: Kier Holmes, Alice Kitajima, Cricket Riley

Cricket Riley is a landscape designer who specializes in lush, low-water garden design. She started at RBG in 2017 and held a variety of positions, most recently as the Design Services Director. In this role, she led a team of landscape designers helping homeowners embrace regionally climate-appropriate gardens. She was also the primary instructor for RBG's Dry Garden Design Certificate Program, which she co-created with Alice Kitajima in 2020.

Alice Kitajima's profound connection to gardens and landscape design started at an early age, thanks to the influence of her father, who immigrated to Los Angeles to install Japanese-style gardens. She has worked at various botanical gardens and arboreta around the United States after finishing her forestry and music studies at University of California, Berkeley. As the Program Director at the Ruth Bancroft Garden, overseeing the education department, her greatest passion was connecting and deepening people's connections with plants.

Kier Holmes is a Bay Area native who, when not digging in her own laboratory-like garden, designing thoughtful gardens for clients, or lecturing on various gardening topics, is a contributing writer and content creator for *Gardenista* and *Sonoma Magazine*. Kier has also contributed to numerous other publications including *Martha Stewart*, *Sunset*, *Better Homes & Gardens*, *National Geographic Kids*, *Edible Marin & Wine Country*, and *Marin Magazine*, plus she is the author of *The Garden Refresh: How to Give Your Yard Big Impact on a Small Budget*.